MUSIC *in*
The Global Village

John Wesley Hildreth

Illustrated By

Christopher John Hildreth

Linus
Publications

Published by Linus Publications, Inc.

Deer Park, NY 11729

ISBN: 1-60797-027-9

Printed in the United States of America.

Print Number 5   4   3   2   1

Dedication

We dedicate this book

with love to my wife Gail,

to David, Bryan, Laura, Ethan and Ian,

and to the memory of my parents, Rozaline and Charles Hildreth.

Table of Contents

Chapter 3

Chapter 4

Chapter 5

Chapter 6

Chapter 7

Chapter 8

Chapter 9

Chapter 12

Chapter References

General Bibliography

Glossary

Index

Preface

In the study of world music we often use the analogy of the *global village* as well as the analogy of the *global orchestra*. The world continues to grow smaller and closer together, so to speak, as the ease of world travel and world communication increases. It is now possible to travel from end of the globe to the other in just a matter of a few hours. Like wise we can access almost any place on the globe almost instantaneously by simply pressing a button. Thus our interaction and relationship with our neighbors around the globe can likened to the closeness of living in a village. Given the interconnectedness and interdependedness of neighbors in the global village, we are obliged to learn as much as possible about our global village and about the marvelous variety of music to be found therein. The urgency of such a learning learning process is underscored by David McAllester, a noted ethnomusicologist who states:

> *We are all citizens of the same small globe. We have the responsibility of this citizenship thrust upon us, willy-nilly, and one of the first of these is to try to understand each other before it is loo late.*
>
> *My studies in world music have brought extraordinary enrichment into my life. I have been to visit other parts of the world as a participant, rather than a tourist. An increased understanding of the arts has broadened my appreciation of everything in my world.*

The major goal of this text is to allow us to go in the spirit of McAllester to visit our neighbors in the global village in heart and mind as participants, and as seekers and learners to approach music in the global village in an informed and appreciative manner with respect for the validity and raison d'etre of musical traditions radically different from our own. [1]

In addition to providing a brief survey of indigenous music of the various regions of the world, it will help students to learn to approach music from a global perspective, to appreciate diverse cultural traditions, and to discover the common denominators found in the music of various cultures, with a view toward understanding and appreciating the interdependedness and interconnectedness of the human family. In so doing, the student will become acquainted with some of the problems, questions, and issues involved in cross-cultural studies of music, and also with some of the theories, methodologies, and concepts associated with ethnomusicology.

---

1. William P. Malm, "Music as a Non-International Universal," National Center For The Performing Arts Quarterly Journal (Bombay), Vol. 3, No. 4, December 1974, 35.

And finally it is hoped that the student will come to understand the impact of cultural diffusion, acculturation, syncretism, and other processes of change, particularly the results of modernization and Westernization. One final and essential goal is to explore new and alternative methods of criticism and evaluation deemed appropriate for the musics of non-Western cultures.

About the Author and Illustrator

John W. Hildreth is a native of Evansville, Indiana. He began his musical studies there with Eva Crawford Brooks with whom he studied piano and who was his inspiration for becoming an organist. He entered the Preparatory School of Music at the University of Evansville as a scholarship student while a student at Lincoln High School. There he studied piano with Margaret Shepherd and organ with Gerald Clark. In 1959 he won the Arion Music Award at Lincoln High School where he played trombone in the band and was drum major during his high school years.

He began his college education at Concordia Junior College in Milwaukee, Wisconsin where he was a member of the college chorus, the brass choir, and was choir tour accompanist and chapel organist, while at the same time pursuing Pre-theological Studies and earning the A.A. Degree. He continued at Concordia Senior College in Fort Wayne, Indiana where he continued his Pre-Theological Studies and chose music as an academic concentration and served as chapel organist. He received the B.A. Degree from Concordia in 1965.

In 1967 he began studies with Professor Robert Reuter at Chicago Musical College, Roosevelt University, Chicago, Illinois in organ and church music and also studied piano with Felix Ganz. He was regularly on the Dean's List and was the recipient of numerous music scholarships. He received a B.M. Degree in Organ and Church Music in 1969 and an M.M. Degree in Organ and Church music with Highest Honors in 1970 from Roosevelt.

He began his doctoral work at the Northwestern University School of Music in Evanston, Illinois and completed the Ph.D. in Musicology and Ethnomusicology in 1978 under the direction of William Porter, Theodore Karp, Aarond Parsons, and Klaus Wachsmann. He also studied piano with Francis Larimer and harpsichord with Dorothy Lane while at Northwestern.

Dr. Hildreth has served as organist and choirmaster at various places, including Augustana College where he served as chapel organist for a number of years. He served as organist and choirmaster at Trinity Episcopal Church in Rock Island, Illinois, Trinity Episcopal Cathedral in Davenport, Iowa, and presently serves as Director of Music at All Saints Episcopal Church in Moline, Illinois. He is on the faculty of the Music Department at Augustana College in Rock Island, Illinois where he has completed 37 years of teaching and holds the rank of full professor. He has taught courses in the History and Literature of Western Music, Music Theory, Music in General Studies, History of American Music, African-American Music, Women in Music, the Art of Listening, and Music in Worldwide

Perspective and World Music, courses in Ethnomusicology, and has published his own materials for teaching in these areas.

Christopher John Hildreth, son of the author, is eighteen years old and is a senior and an honor student at Rock Island High School. Unlike his father, he is extremely knowledgeable of and proficient with computers, and his skills have been inestimable in the preparation of this book. He also began studying piano at the tender age of four and has brought those skills to the preparation of the manuscript as well. He was awarded the honor of participating in the IS Explorers Program, an honors computer program offered by the John Deere Corporation in Moline, Illinois. He plans to matriculate at Augustana College in the fall of 2010 and is interested in majoring in Computer Science or some combination of Earth Sciences. One of his career interests is in computers and video design. Another career interest is in pilot training in the Air Force after college.

Acknowledgements

I am deeply indebted to so many for their assistance, contributions, and encouragement in writing this book. To my many excellent teachers and mentors, particularly Klaus Wachsmann, Bruno Nettl, William Malm, Theodore Karp, Aarond Parsons, Wiliam Porter, Robert Reuter, and so many others who planted the seeds and helped prepare me for a fruitful career in the teaching of world music.

I am immeasurably indebted to my son Christopher who has brought his considerable computer skills to this project and has aided greatly in the the photographic realization of musical instruments, the index, and other illustrations throughout the book. Thanks also to Egan Maginis, another high school student, who provided the artwork for the cover.

A special thanks also to Mr. Xione Bau Tian, visiting Artist-in-Residence from China, who graciously consented to the detailed interview included in Chapter 6. To Greg Swanson and Subhasis Mukherjeeof SPANDAN, (a not-for-profit organization dedicated to promoting awareness and appreciation of North Indian Classical Music in the upper-Midwest region) who taught us by bringing to us such outstanding artists as Ruchira Panda and Professor Sanjoy Bandopadhyay, and from whom we continue to learn much about world music traditions. A special thanks also to Mr. and Mrs. Cecil Cook who offered their Korean instruments for photographing.

To my many students and colleagues who have accompanied me on the journey of learning and teaching and who have inspired me in ways neither they nor I could have imagined, I express my sincere gratitude and appreciation.

And finally, to my family, colleagues, and friends for their forbearance, confidence, and support, I offer my sincere thanks.

CHAPTER 1

Organology

Instruments of the Global Orchestra

Musical instruments are viewed the world over in many different ways. The word *organology* which is used in reference to classifying musical instruments is perhaps an acknowledgement that objects that have come to be used as musical instruments evolved from implements, tools and utensils *(organon)* quite apart from any intended musical function. Like the tools and implements from which they evolved, "musical instruments are extensions of man's body: they expand extend, broaden his music-making potential, increase (but not always) his range of forms or expression, delight his ears with new timbres and sound, make possible technical feats (lightning-fast notes or thunderous earthshaking loud-ness, for example) that seem to free him from his bodily limits like the wings of a bird lifting it from the everyday confines and dangers of the earth[1]". Primitive persons moved beyond their bodies (hand-clapping, foot-stomping, beating upon the chest, abdomen, thighs, or buttocks) to the aforementioned extensions.

Supernatural power and magic have been associated with musical instruments throughout history. It has been believed by many that spirits dwell within musical instruments as indicated in a work by Curt Scahs entitled Geist und Werden der Musikinstrumente (The Spirit and Being or Development of Musical Instruments). Sexual symbolism and musical instruments are intimately connected in many cultures. And ways of classifying musical instruments "are often synopses-or terse accounts of a culture's, subculture's, or individual's deep-seated ideas about music and instruments, as well as, in some cases, philosophical, religious, and social beliefs[2]. Many scholars of non-Western music have come to realize that "instruments are not just static objects but are products of human

---

1. David Reck, Music of the Whole Earth (New York: Charles Scribner's Sons, 1977), 44.

2. Margaret J. Kartomi, On Concepts and Classifications of Musical Instruments, (Chicago: University of Chicago Press. 1990), 7.

culture and therefore resemble living organisms and are subject to continual change both in their parts and as a whole." [3]

There is much to be learned about cultures studied in the context of all aspects of civilization, but perhaps no more satisfactorily than through a study of the origin and dissemination of musical instruments. Two positions are commonly held with respect to these two issues. One is the monogenetic position which holds that all types of musical instruments had a common origin from which all similar instruments had a common from which all similar instruments evolved. The second position, the polygenetic one, holds that similar instruments had multiple origins and continued to multiply and spread across the earth. The most plausible position seems to be the monogenetic one. Along with folk songs, musical instruments are probably some of the most "indefatigable tourists" in existence. Like folksongs they have certainly been subject to countless alterations, but in spite of the many variants, have maintained recognizable characteristics which link them to earlier prototypes.

Given these realizations, it is quite incorrect to assume that the categories used in reference to instruments of the Western orchestra are appropriate for the study and classification of non-Western instruments. To do so would impose cultural assumptions quite inappropriately on the music and musical instruments of non-Western cultures. Curt Sachs said of the Western classification of strings, winds, and percussion, that "we might as well divide Americans into Californians, bankers, and Catholics."[4] He viewed it as illogical and lacking in comprehensiveness and a consistent principle of division. His reasoning was that "the usual division of the of the orchestra into stringed, wind and percussion instruments is based on three different principles instead of one: the sonorous material acted upon in 'strings'; the activating force in 'wind'; and the action itself in 'percussion.'"[5] Of the many classificatory schemes devised throughout the nineteenth and twentieth centuries, the Sachs-Hornbostel is the one most widely used by scholars today. While not perfect, the system is open-ended and suitable for classifying instruments the world over.

By way of comparison, the standard method of classifying the instruments of the Western orchestra, which is an expanded and modified version of the Western tripartite system known to Sachs, will now be presented, followed by a reduced and modified form of the Sachs-Hornbostel classification.

Instruments of the Western Orchestra

Musical instruments of the Western orchestra have over time evolved and have become more refined and technically sophisticated. These instruments are generally classified into four main groups or families, namely. strings, woodwinds,

---

3.   Ibid., 31.

4.   Kartomi, <u>On Concepts and Classifications of Musical instruments.</u> 162.

5.   Ibid., 167-168.

brass, and percussion The most common instruments found in these categories are as follows:

STRINGS
Violin
Viola
Cello
Double Bass

WOODWINDS
Piccolo
Flute
Clarinet
Bass Clarinet
Saxophone
Oboe
English Horn
Bassoon
Contrabassoon

BRASS
Trumpet
French
Horn
Trombone
Euphonium

PERCUSSION
Baritone Tuba
Snare Drum
Bass Drum
Timpani
Tambourine
Cymbals
Triangle
Gong
Castanets
Chimes
Xylophone
Piano

There are, of course, other percussion instruments, but those shown above are most commonly used in the Western orchestra. The harp is another string instrument used almost exclusively in orchestral settings. There are other string instruments which are more often used in other than orchestral settings, such as popular, rock, folk, and others. These would include the acoustic guitar, electric guitar, banjo, and Mandolin.

There are keyboard instruments which have enjoyed popularity in the Western world. The harpsichord and celeste are sometimes found in orchestral settings. The organ appears less frequently in orchestral or ensemble settings while the celeste is quite often found in such settings.

Photo by Charles Phelps Gushing

Technological advances now provide us with new instruments of the synthesizer/computer type, which are capable of producing a greater variety of tones, timbres, and which are capable or revolutionizing practically every aspect of composing, performing and music making.

The classificatory system shown above seems adequate for the instruments of the Western orchestra, however, it is not very useful for classifying instruments around the world. In order to learn something about musical instruments in other parts of the world, we now turn to another way of classifying musical instruments. The following is an introduction to and a brief summary of the Sachs-Hornboste Classification System. See Curt Sachs, <u>The History of Musical Instuments</u> (New York: W.Norton & Co., Inc. 1940)

Idiophones

These *self-sounding* instruments consist of naturally sonorous material which when vibrated creates sound without the aid of strings, membranes or other attachments. Idiophones originated from extensions of handclapping and the stamping of feet.

Eight different sub-classes of idiophones according to the way vibrations are set in motion:

- Struck

- Struck together

- Stamped

- Stamping

- Shaken

- Scraped

- Plucked

- Rubbed or Friction

Membranophones

These instruments make their sounds when a tightly-stretched skin or membrane is made to vibrate. This category includes most drums in existence with the exception of slit drums which have no membranes and must therefore be classified as idiophones. They are further classified according to a description of the following features:

1. Material	4. Fastening of skins
2. Shape	5. Playing position
3. Skin or head	6. Manner of playing

Aerophones

The air itself is the vibrator in these instruments. For this reason they are usually called wind instruments or air instruments. The sub-classes of aerophones are:

1. Straight/Plain tubes and pipes

2. Reeds
   Clarinet (Single-reed)
   Oboe (Double-reed)

3. Free

Free aerophones make their sounds without enclosing a column of air in a tube or pipe, such as the Native-American eagle bone whistle or the bull-roarer.

Chordophones

Chordophones are instruments with cords or strings stretched between fixed points. The strings may be struck with sticks, plucked with the bare fingers or a plectron or plectrum, or bowed or sounded by wind. The stringed instruments can be reduced to four fundamental types.

1.   ZITHER

     A zither has no neck or yoke. The strings are stretched between two ends of a body, whether this body *is* a resonator itself or whether it requires an attached resonator. A few types are listed below:

     - Stick

     - Tube

     - Board

     - Long Zither

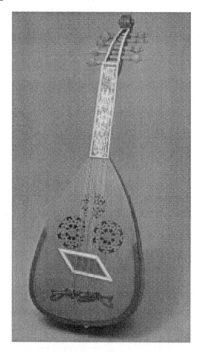

2.   LUTE

     A lute is composed of a body, and of a neck, which serves both as a handle and as a means of stretching the string(s) beyond the body.

3.   LYRE

     A lyre has a body with a yoke in place of a neck, that is, two arms projecting upward, the upper ends of which are connected by acrossbaf. The strings are stretched over a soundboard and are fastened at a crossbar at the top. They are either plucked or bowed.

4.   HARP

     The harp is the only instrument in which the plane of the strings is vertical, not parallel, to the soundboard; the strings are attached to the soundboard, but run vertically away from it, and not along it.

The Chinese Classification

One non-Western culture, the Chinese, has a system of classifying instruments according to <u>eight sounds</u>. These sounds are called the <u>pa yin</u>. In this system, the instruments are classified according to the material they are made of. The materials are as follows:

Bamboo

Gourd

Metal

Silk

Stone

Earth (pottery)

Wood

Skin

Examples of instruments belonging to these categories are as follows:

-Bamboo	p'ai hsiao	(panpipes)
	ti tzu	(flute)
	hsiao	(flute)
-Gourd	sheng	(mouth organ)
-Metal	yang ch'in	(dulcimer with metal strings)
	yun lo	(metal hammered gong)
	hao t'ung	(metal trumpet)
	la pa	(metal trumpet)
	pien chung	(metal tuned bells)
-Silk	erh hsien	(violin with two silk strings)
	hu chin	(violin with four silk strings)
	p' i p'a	(guitar with four silk strings)
	san hsien	(guitar with three silk strings,'
	ch ' in	(seven-string zither)
	cheng	(thirteen-stringed zither)

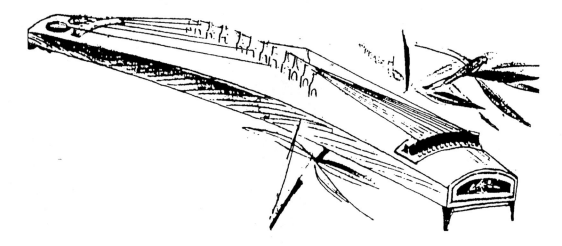

-Earth (pottery)	husuan	(clay ocarina)
-Wood	yu or o	(a crouching tiger, scraped idiophone)
	chu	(box thumped with a pole)
-Stone	pien k'ing	(stone chimes)
	ch' ing	(stone chimes)
-Skin	chin-ku	(drum)
	ying ku	(drum)
	tsu ku	(drum)
	po fu	(drum)
	t'ao ku	(drum)
	pang ku	(drum)

As with any classification, not all entries can be expected to fit comfortably. A case in point would be the so na, which, because it is a wooden pipe with a reed mouthpiece and a copper bell, would seem to require some kind of composite classification at the very least.

The Pan-Islamic Crescent

(Arabic Music)

الموسيقى العربية

(Egyptian Music)
(Heiroglyphics)

(Persian Music)

موسيقى فارسى

(Hebrew Music)

מוסיקה עברית

CHAPTER 2

The Pan-Islamic Crescent

North Africa and the Middle East

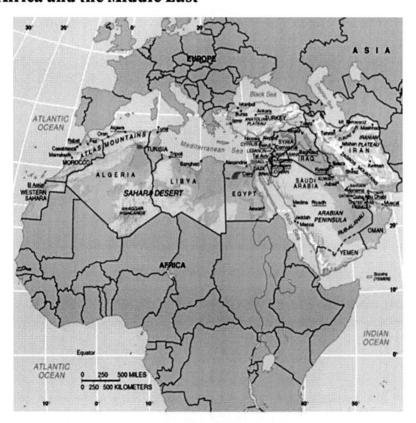

African music like the continent of Africa itself, is a vast and multifaceted phenomenon. It is in no wise possible to speak of African music in any all-inclusive sense. Just as there are many different languages and culture groups in Africa, there are countless musical styles and practices on that continent.

On either side of the Sahara, one is able to discern a rather distinct and pronounced difference in the musical styles and practices.

North of the Sahara there is a strong Moslem influence, with musical practices being more akin to Arab/Oriental types of music. The classical, folk, and popular music of the societies of North Africa, the Arabized communities in the northern Sudan, various areas in the Maghreb, and the shore of East Africa are not indicative of traditional African music, but belong to the Arab/Oriental family of modal music.[1] Charles Duvelle, in a work entitled "Oriental Music in Black Africa," cites the characteristics of Arab-influenced African music:

1) varied modal scales, sometimes pentatonic, heptatonic, anhemitonic, and often employing microtonal intervals;

2) rhythmic-metrical quality can be clearly felt, unlike the elusive polyrhthms of sub-Sarahan Africa;

3) abundant use of ornamentation;

4) musical instruments (most common);

   a) lutes with one or more strings

   b) one-stringed fiddles

   c) hour-glass drum with adjustable skins

   d) transverse flutes

   e) conical oboe

   f) long metal trumpets

   g) sistrums

5) preferred and most-used texture is homophony.[2]

---

1.   J. H. K. Nketia, <u>The Music of Africa</u> (New York: W. W. Norton and Co. , Inc., 1974), 3.

2.   Charles Duvelle, <u>African Music</u>, Papers read at a meeting organized by UNESCO in Yaounde, Cameroon, 23-27 February, 1970   (7 Place Saint Sulpice, Paris: La Revue Musicale, 1972).

The above must not be viewed as an inflexible list of parameters to be rigidly applied to all Moslem-influenced African music, for as William Malm points out, the acceptance of Islam does not necessarily mean the total destruction of indigenous traditions. At the terminals of the Sahara caravan routes, there are many Negroid groups that either maintain two separate musical traditions or show a mixture. The Wolofs of Senegal and Gambia, for example, show a mixture. They use cylindrical and potshaped, singleheaded drums in groups to produce polyrhythms for their secular dances. When, however, their holy man sings Moslem hymns (hasida), a small kettle drum called a tabala is used, along with an iron beater. Together they produce simple single rhythms much more akin to the music of the rest of the Moslem world. In the Sudan and Ethiopia, where the racial mixture is extensive, a great variety of bowed lutes and monophonic songs is found, as well as lyres that recall the more ancient cultures of Egypt. In Ethiopia, the situation is further complicated by a strong Coptic Christian tradition, not to mention the Falasha Jews. The Copts use stone bells, dowel, and sing in melismatic chant style that intrigues the ear with its Christian-Moslem mixture.[3]

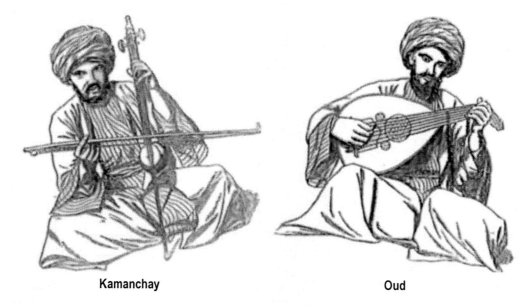

Kamanchay   Oud

Arabic Influence Throughout The Pan-islamic Crescent

Arabia shares borders with Iraq and Jordan in the north, the Gulf of Oman and the Persian Gulf on the east, the Gulf of Adan and the Arabian Sea in the south, and with the Gulf of Aqaba and the Red Sea on the west. The largest and most populous state in Arabia today is of course Saudi Arabia. Other Arab states include the united Arab Emirates, Kuwait, Qatar, Yemen, Oman, Bahrain, and other neutral zones. [4]

---

3.   William P. Malm, Music Cutures of the Pacific, the Near East, and Asia (Englewood Cliffs, New Jersey: Prentice-Hall. Inc.. 1967), 38

4.   William H. Harris and Judith S. Levey, The New Columbia Encyclopedia, (New York: Columbia University Press,   1975), 130-131.

Arabic languages derive from the Hamito-Semitic family of languages and are a part of the South Semitic group of the Semitic subdivision of that family. Arabic can be found throughout the Pan-Islamic Crescent including North Africa, Iraq, Jordan, Syria, Israel, Lebanon, Malta, Mauritania, Chad, and in at least seventeen other countries in Africa and Asia where at least 100 million people speak the language. Wherever Islam has manifested itself, Arabic has followed, due to the fact that it is the sacred language of Islam and the Koran, its holy book. [5]

Saudi Arabia

Arabic influence runs deep in the music of the Pan-Islamic Crescent. The scalar-melodic melodic material in Arabic music is derived from modes called *maqam* or *maqamat* (plural) which exist in various forms. These modes, like the ragas of India and the dastgahs of Persian music, are more than scales. They are also a blueprint, a procedure or a form of melody-making which serves as the basis for creating or improvising. These types are somewhat like the Greek modes in that they are thought to embody various moods, such as happiness, loneliness, tranquility, heroism, and so on. In addition to their ascending and descending forms, these types are highly embellished and contain many microtones and other subtleties, which along with their extra-musical considerations makes them rather interesting and often complex sources of melodic material. [6]

It will be shown that Arabic instruments are shared throughout the Pan-Islamic Crescent. The names of the instruments, like the names of the modes may be different, but the instruments are essentially the same as are the modes in their construction and function.

---

5. *The Arab World, Its Music and Its People.* (Desto Album I) 504; *1969)*. 2.

6. Ibid., 3

   Arabic instruments that will be encountered throughout the Pan-Islamic Crescent are the darabukkah, oud, rebab, nay, kanoun, santur, cembalon, kemengeh, and arghoul.

Tombak/Darabuka

Nay

Mijwiz

Arghool

EGYPT

The Arab Republic of Egypt is in Northeast Africa Lower Egypt consists of the Nile Delta and Upper Egypt spreads south from Cairo, the capital. The land Is extremely dry and without rain. Without the flow of the Nile, life would be difficult, if not impossible. Egypt is one of the oldest civilizations in the world and was one of the most powerful for many centuries.[7]

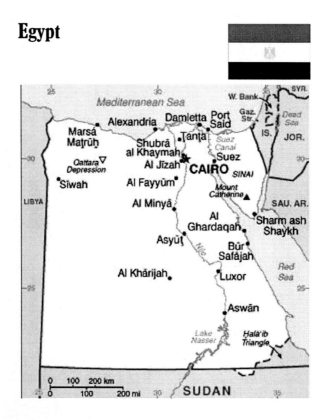

Egyptian music can be traced back to at least 5,000 years due to a rich repository of iconographical and literary sources. Such aerophones as pipes and flutes and chordophones of the harp and lyre variety are represented. Ancient idiophones such as clappers, cymbals, and sistrums have been found and preserved. Although often associated with ancient Egypt, the lyres and harps may not have been indigenous, but were probably imported from Asia.

There are a number of distinct regional folk music styles. In the eastern and western deserts are the Berbers who use drums of ancient derivation. The population of the Southern Nile valley is mainly Arabic. Their music is generally pentatonic. An aerophone called the mizmar is prevalent along with a variety of drums.

---

7. Harris, Levey, 838-839.

Egyptian cithara

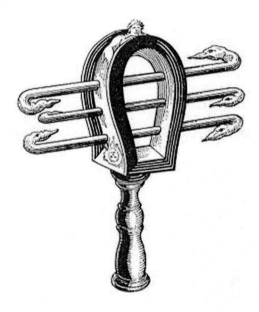

Sistrum

The delta region of the Nile features music which uses a heptatonic scale rather than the pentatonic. Like much of the music in the Middle East, this music emphasizes microtonal inflection. Two aerophones, the mizmar (oboe) and the arghul (double pipes with single reeds) are prevalent. A membranophone called the tabla baladi (drum with two heads) is used.

The Nubians of Southern Egypt have a language and musical style that is distinct. Like the Arab populations in the southern Nile valley, their music is pentatonic rather than heptatonic as it is in the Nile delta region. Two of their instruments are the tambura (five-stringed lyre) and the tar (large drum).[8]

8. Oriental Music Festival, School of Oriental Studies, Elvet Hill, Durham. England.

TURKEY

Turkey

The republic of Turkey is situated in Asia minor and SE Europe and shares borders with Iraq, Syria, Greece, Bulgaria, Russia and Iran. The majority of the population speaks Turkish with small minorities speaking Kurdish, Arabic, Circasian, Greek, Armenian, Georgian, and Laze. Likewise the majority of the population is Muslim (99%) with small pockets of Orthodox Christians, Roman Catholics, Protestants, and Jews who speak Spanish.

Turkey has an extensive musical history with musical influences from bordering countries in Central Asia, Persian and Arab influences, and influences Islamic musical practices which resulted from the adoption of Islam by the Turks.

Both classical and folk music traditions flourish in Turkey. Instruments of the classical tradition include the following:

<u>Aerophone</u>

ney	-	end-blown flute

<u>Chordophones</u>

santur	-	dulcimer
kanun	-	plucked zither
tanbur	-	long-necked lute
rebab	-	fiddle

<u>Membranophone</u>

def	-	frame drum

There are two instrumental forms in the classical tradition, namely *pesrev* and *saz semai*, consisting of four movements each with varying interludes.

Instruments of the folk tradition include the following:

Aerophones

    zurna   -   shawm

    tulum   -   bagpipe

Chordophones

    saz   -   long-necked lute

    keman   -   western violin

Mebranophone

    def   -   frame drum [9]

There are many types of folksongs which most often are unaccompanied. The metrical structure of the poetic texts greatly influences musical form and structure.

Rhythm in Turkish music is rich and varied. Unlike regular meters in European music, asymmetrical meters of five, seven and eleven beats with irregular subdivisions are common with the addition of syncopation and dotted rhythms. Turkish rhythms have been attractive to many western composers including Mozart and Beethoven. Turkish rhythms were heard by westerners when Turkish Janissary Bands were marching through parts of Europe. A common adaptation of these rhythms was called *alla turca*.

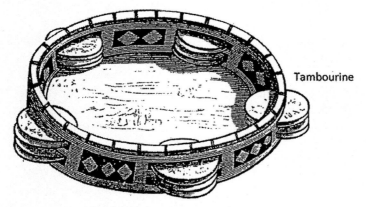

Tambourine

Dover Pictorial Archive Series

---

9. Oriental Music Festival School of Oriental Studies, Blvet Hill. Durham. England.

IRAN

Prior to 1935, Iran was known as Persia. Iran is the second largest country in the Middle East and shares borders with Russia, Afghanistan, Pakistan, the Gulf of Oman and the Persian Gulf, Turkey and Afghanistan. Ethnic diversity in Iran includes Kurds, Lurs, Qashqai, Bakhtiari, Turks, Tartars, and Arabs. The predominant religion is Islam (98%) but there are also pockets of Zoroastrians and Assyrian and Armenian Christians, a few Roman Catholics, Protestants, and Jews. Manichaeism and Mithraism are also religious movements that originated in Iran.[10]

One learns classical music by embracing the radif which consists of a collection of ancient pieces which make up a classical repertoire. The pieces of the radif are arranged in twelve groups. Seven of these groups are known as primary dastgahs. Gushe refers the individual pieces found in each of the twelve dastgahs. The seven principal dastgahs make up the basic modal structure of Iranian classical music with the remaining five being used derivatively or as secondary dastgahs.

The gushes, like scalar-melodic material in other musics, provide modal, melodic, and perhaps rhythmic material upon which the performer is obliged to improvise. There is a good bit of flexibility in the majority of gushes, however, there are some gushes which are metrically regulated, offering unity within diversity. Triple and duple meters are common in classical music while asymmetric meters are most often found in folk music. [11]

---

10. Harris. Levey, 1359.
11. Oriental Musical Festival.

Iranian music is principally melodic and therefore does not boast of a systematic harmonic system. The music is derived first of all from the radif, is then enhanced by the skeletal formulae offered by various gushe, which when coupled with the freedom and flexibility offered therein, offer an endless source of musical expression.

Reference has been made to an augmented second in this music which might be more correctly viewed as a neutral second in that it falls somewhere between a major and minor second in western terms. Perhaps it is best stated that the interval of a second is highly flexible and perhaps indeterminate.

Aerophones and chordophones are among the most popular instruments in Iran.

Aerophones

      nay   -   (generic term for flutes)

Chordophones

      ude   -   (9-11 string lute)

      tar   -   (six strings, plucked)

      setar   -   (4 strings)

      santur   -   (hammered dulcimer using wooden mallets)

One of the difficulties in understanding Middle Eastern music is the ambivalence toward music due to the prophet Mohammed's injunction against music, particularly in mosques. This has not inhibited music but rather has led to ways of reconciling music with such injunctions. The ambivalence toward music is so pronounced that even the word for music is of Persian and Greek origin *(musiqi)*. Even then there is a bifurcation of the concept in Iran which renders the concept as both *khandan* and *musiqi* which are at opposite ends of a continuum. *Khandan* embraces music that is sacred, improvised, non-metric, vocal, and performed solo. *Musiqi* on the other hand refers to music that is secular, composed, metric, instrumental, and played by an ensemble. *Khandan,* meaning "to recite" has as its purest expression reading from the Quran, the most acceptable and least objectionable expression, while at the other end of the continuum *(musiqi)* would be found such things as instrumental music for belly dancing, the most objectionable and least acceptable in strict Islamic terms. In between these two poles can be found various forms of chanted epic poetry and other vocal and instrumental combinations.[12]

The status of musicians is also intriguing in that amateur musicians have a higher status than professional musicians. The scholarly study of music, because of its association with language, is regarded more highly. The freedom to improvise as they wish gives amateur musicians a higher status than professional musicians who must work according to the dictates of their patrons. Many professional musicians are minorities and non-Muslim which accords them a lower status.[13]

---

12. Bruno Nettl, *"Music in the Middle East",* Excursions in World Music (Upper Saddle River, New Jersey: Pearson-Prentice Hall, 2008), 67.
13. Ibid.,69-70.

IRAQ

Modern-day Iraq derives from ancient Mesopotamia. It shares borders with Turkey, Iraq, and Saudi Arabia. Arabic is the predominant language spoken in Iraq, and Shiite and Sunni Muslims are the predominant religious group. Minority groups include Turks, Assyrians and Kurds. From the 8th century until around 1258 AD, Baghdad had the distinction of being the capital of the Arab-Islamic Caliphate, making it a stronghold of Arabic culture and music. Even after the fall of the Caliphate empire, Arabic influence continued to flourish in Iraq, but also the neighboring states of Turkey, Persia and India. [14]

Although most Arab music was originally vocal as we have seen in our discussion of Islamic influence on the music, it is not unusual to find percussion and other instrumental accompaniment to songs in Iraq. A common Arabic instrument, the oud, is often used for this purpose. Religious intonations such as Qur'an reading and the Call to Prayer remained unaccompanied.

As in most Pan-Islamic music, there is a considerable amount of embellishment, and rhythms, when used, are often complex. And like most Middle Eastern music, it is largely melodic with no emphasis on harmony or counterpoint.

14. Harris, Levey, 1361.

In Iraq, as in Iran, students learn from their teacher who painstakingly guides them through a body of music over a long period, carefully examining each maqam, "explaining and demonstrating to the student what is essential, obligatory, and optimal." [15]

Music accompanies social, secular, and religious events. As in most cultures, every aspect of the life cycle engages music in one way or another, such as birth, marriage, death and the like.

Iraqi music has a long history dating back to the ancient Sumerians and Babylonians. Throughout time, Iraq has been influenced by the coming of Islam and by its Greek, Persian, Turkish and Indian neighbors. Mass media, modernization and Westernization, as well as other influences have influenced Iraqi music. This influence can be seen in local instruments being replaced by Western instruments and other instruments from outside the region, and also in the gradual relaxation in both secular and religious practices. [16]

---

15. Bruno Nettl *"Music in the Middle East"*, Excursions in World Music (Upper Saddle River, New Jersey: Pearson-Prentice Hall, 2008).

16. Oriental Music Festival.

AFGHANISTAN

Afghanistan shares borders with China, India, Pakistan, Iran, and Asiatic Russia. Its name means the Land of the Afghans. Its original name was *Khorasan,* which means *"the land from which the sun rises."* Almost all of the people are Muslim, the greater majority being Sunni while the remaining minority is Shiite. Persian and Pushtu (Afghan) are the main spoken languages. [17]

Afghanistan

Afghanistan's location puts it directly in the path of important conquest and commerce routes thus making it important in linking Asia and Europe together. Given its borders, Afghanistan is host to a number of influences from different directions. In the east the music is heavily Hindu-oriented, while in the west and the north Central Asian and Near Eastern styles predominate. Mongolian and Siberian influences are to be noted as well. As a result of migrations through conquest and commerce routes, there are pockets of minority groups throughout the land, each with its unique traditions. [18]

As in most Islamic-influenced cultures, the predominant musical style is vocal with emphasis on the chanting of religious texts from the Qur'an and the Call to Worship. Next in importance is the setting of poetic texts to music.

---

17. William P. Malm, <u>Music Cultures of the Pacific, Near East, and Asia</u>, 3rd Ed., (Upper Saddle River, NJ: Prentice-Hall, 1996) 113.

18. Ibid., 114.

The usual Islamic ambivalence toward music obtains in Afghanistan as well. Religious concerns also governs gender roles and the participation of women in music. Women are restricted to such instruments as the jaw's harp and the tambourine and are never to perform in public, let alone participate in dancing.

The following are some of the more common and shared instruments. These instruments show the many influences impacting the musics and cultures of this region. The geographical and ethnic affiliations will accompany the description of the instruments and should aid in unraveling a complex variety of instruments.

Chordophones

robab	short-necked fretted lute	Pashtuns	Afghanistan
tanbur	long-necked lute, frets, melodic and drone strings	Pashtuns	Afghanistan
dambura	long-necked lute, strings, frets two	Uzbeks Tajiks	Northern Afghanistan
dutar	long-necked lute, two strings, frets	Uzbeks Turkmen	Uzbek Turkestan
robab	six-stringed lute	Pamir	Central Asia
dombra	lute	Kazakh	Central Asia
dutar	lute	Herati	Iran
sarinda	bowed lute	Pashtun Baluch	North India
vaj, wafi	arched harp	Kafir	Nuristan

Aerophones

tuiduk, nal, nai	long, open, end-blown flutes	Turkmen Nuristan	Turkmen Nuristan
dili-tuiduk	single-reed pipes	Turkmen	Turkestan
surnai	double-reed pipes	Widespread	Afghanistan
ushpulak	animal-shaped whistles	Children	Afghanistan

Membranophones

doira, daria, daf	large tambourine	Women	Middle Eastern
zirbaghali	vase-shaped, single headed drum, under the arm	Men	Middle Eastern

dohl	two-headed drum	Pashtuns	India
tabla-baya	set of drums	Radio music	North India
ghergheranak	ratchet, two-headed drum with attached beaters	Children	Afghanistan

Idiophones

chang changko'uz	metal jaw's harp	Widespread	Persia Uzbek
zang, tal, tusak	small finger cymbals	Widespread	Persia Uzbek
zang-i kaftar	small metal rhythmic Instruments	Lutenists	North Regions

In Afghanistan today, two musical directions exist side by side. On the one hand there is the local, recognizable music that is deemed acceptable, and on the other hand there is the newer music that is influenced by modernization (the radio), international influences and a relaxation of the constraints on artistic freedom. [19]

---

19. Slobin, Mark. "Afghanistan." The New Grove Dictionary of Music and Musicians, ed. Stanley Sadie. (New York: McMillan Publishers Ltd., 1980). 137-138.

JEWISH MUSIC

Any discussion of Jewish music must necessarily reference the Bible, particularly The Old Testament, wherein are contained countless references to music among the Hebrews. This will necessarily enhance our overall understanding of ancient music in the Middle East. Remnants of those ancient traditions are still very much alive today. We see this in present-day usage of the shofar (ram's horn). Many other instruments are mentioned in The Old Testament which are no longer used today. Mention is also made of great personages in Biblical times who were associated with music, such as King David, Saul, Miriam, and Jubal who has been regarded by some as the inventor of music, and many others. Countless Biblical stories have been set to music by great composers throughout the ages, including Handel, Mendelssohn, Benjamin Britten, Arthur Honneger, Ralph Vaughan Williams, Arnold Schoenberg, and many others. [20]

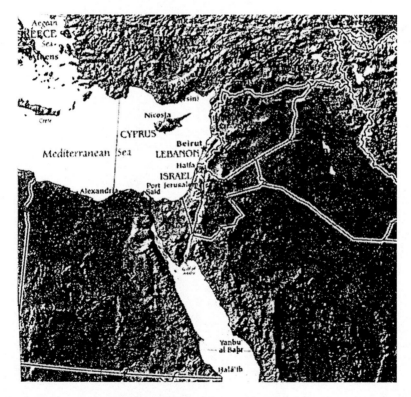

Christian chant is deeply indebted to Jewish chant Traditionally Jewish music centered on incantations and invocations and prayers of various types. Today music varies according to the level of orthodoxy or reformed character of a given local congregation. Nevertheless, Jewish music has retained a rather unified character in its religious setting in spite of the diasporan nature of their history. A few adaptations of Christian music are allowed by more liberal

---

20. Alan Blackwood, "Music in the Bible," <u>Music of the World</u> (Englewood Cliffs, New Jersey: Prentice-Hall, Inc., 1991)36-37.

groups, and likewise Christians have made use of Jewish melodies in their hymns. [21]

With the establishment in 1948 of the state of Israel and the subsequent return of Jewish populations from around the world, there began to develop a kind of folk and popular music based on the musical styles of Eastern Europe and the Middle East 22 As a result, five stylistic developments can be noted. First, a rather unified liturgical style has been passed down over time. A second style consists of religious poems borrowed from Gentile practice. *Nigun and piyutim* are examples of this style. A third type encompasses secular songs from lands where Jews have sojourned. A fourth type draws on the pan-Islamic style that surrounds the modern state of Israel. A fifth tradition represents an attempt to establish a new secular folk music which draws its inspiration from the mundane struggles of their present existence while at the same time drawing on influences of the surrounding Middle Eastern cultures and more distant cultures (European and Russian) which hosted the Jewish Diaspora. [23]

Jews who settled in Europe were classified in two ways. The Sephardim refers to those Jews who settled in Spain and Portugal. During this sojourn they cultivated a genre called the *romance* or *romancero*. Although it originated during the Renaissance in Spain, it was adapted to the Sephardic language and was sometimes sung with guitar accompaniment. Those Jews who settled in Russia and Central and Eastern Europe were referred to as the Askenazim. Their music maintained more of a Middle Eastern character. [24]

A distinct group of diasporan musicians is the klezmorim which developed out of the Ashkenazic tradition in Russia and Eastern Europe. The instrumentation of these groups includes violins, bass, cimbalon, and a distinctive clarinet. Brass and accordian were later added as was jazz and elements of theater music after its arrival in the United States. [25]

---

21. Charles Hoffer, Music Listening Today. 3rd Ed (Belmont, California : Thomson-Schirmer, 2007), 358.

22. Bruno Nettl, Excursions in World Music 4th Ed.. (Upper Saddle River, New Jersey: Prentice-Hall, 2008), 62-63.

23. William P. Malm. Music Cultures of the Pacific. Near East and Asia, 3rd Ed., (Upper Saddle River, NJ: Prentice-Hall, 1996) 101-102.

24. William Alves, Music of the Peoples of World (Belmont, CA: Thomson-Schirmer, 2006), 101.

25. Ibid., 102.

Sub-Saharan Africa

(Kiswahili reference to music)

Kiswahili Mahewa Flava Ngoma Jusi Muziki

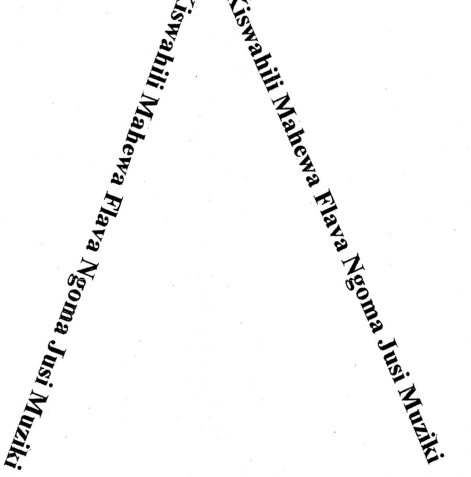

Kiswahili Mahewa Flava Ngoma Jusi Muziki

CHAPTER 3

Sub-Saharan Africa

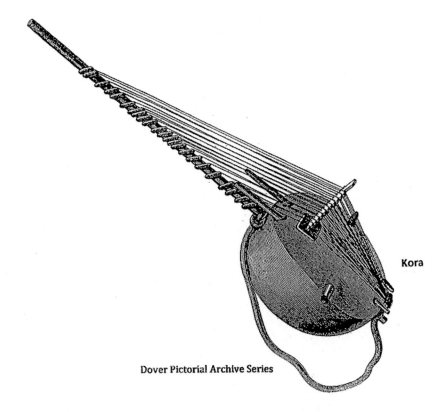

Kora

Dover Pictorial Archive Series

Beyond the Moslem-influenced complications north of the Sahara and along the Sahara caravan routes,there is a vast array of musical styles south of the Sahara. While there are significant differences to be discovered in the music of West, Central, East and South Africa, they are not as vast as the differences between the musical styles of North Africa and music south of the Sahara.

Alan Merriam, while acknowledging the difficulty involved in trying to cite any overall characteristics of sub-Saharan African music which distinguishes it from the Arab/Oriental, Moslem-influenced traditions of the North, nevertheless offers a list of parameters which give a generally clear outline of sub-Saharan music which identifies it as an area with similar musical characteristics throughout. In this regard Merriam describes the following characteristics of sub-Saharan music:

> • • • • <u>an emphasis on rhythmic and metric complexity expressed throughout the musical system; the use of extended syncopation, or off-beat phrasing of melodic accents, as a melodic device; the antiphonal call and response pattern with overlapping between the parts;</u> the presence of <u>two part formal structures;</u> the use of <u>improvisation;</u> the presence of the <u>simultaneous sounding of two or more pitches; a wide variety of tone colors and ornamental devices, including rising attack, falling release, qlissando, and bend and dip; and probably a scale approximating the diatonic.</u> (Italics mine) there are other possible characteristics of African music, including lack of coincidence of main beats in drumming, metronome sense, the conception of musical activity as motor activity, strong attention to proper and accurate tuning of percussion devices, special melodic structures, and various others. [1]

African music has been grossly misunderstood, distorted, and misrepresented by western scholarship. The music is by no means simply a matter of drums and drumming. Although drumming is a most important aspect of African music, one need only look at the large groups of instruments other than membranophones to see that there are many other characteristics to be considered. Klaus Wachsmann points out that musical instruments in African society are far more than "an object for the creation of sound." He sees musical instruments and musical form generally bound up with cultural systems.[2] Wachsmann sees this taking place on at least three levels.

> The level of <u>social function</u> is perhaps most accessible to us in these times of social turmoil. (Italics mine) It is easy to see that an instrument can be said to reinforce the social order in all sorts of ways and that the social order in turn sustains instrumental usage. The second level is concerned with <u>beliefs regarding the nature of the universe,</u> such as the belief in a kind of life force which can be 'administered' by a musical instrument. This is more difficult for general western audiences to grasp, because it is so different from the modern aesthetic which emphasizes entertainment and trivial, nonheard background music. The third level deals with <u>physiological factors which produce a strong bond between instrument and musical</u> forms, and this bond complements the cultural system.[3]

---

1.   Alan P. Merriam, "Characteristics of African Music," <u>International Folk Music Journal</u> (1959), XI, 17.

2.   Klaus P. Wachsmann, "The Interrelations of Musical Instruments, Musical Forms, and Cultural Systems in Africa," <u>Technology and Culture</u>, v/12 (1971), 399.

3.   Ibid.

A most important consideration in African music is the role of music in traditional African society. By traditional African music is meant the indigenous music of Africa of the pre-colonial period or the music which has survived the acculturative impact of non-African cultures.[4] Alan Merriam properly describes the relationship of music to African society when he states that

> . . . one of the characteristics of the African musical system is the stress placed upon musical activity as an integral and functioning part of the society; that is a feature which music shares with other aesthetic aspects of culture in Africa and one which is emphasized in almost all nonliterate societies. Thus music finds expression in the everyday life of the people to a degree probably more fully realized than in western society. And further, more people seem to take an active part in musical activities. Spectators and performers are frequently indistinguishable in a social dance, ceremony, or whatever the occasion might be. . . . Music plays a part, then, in all aspects of culture; in political organization it may stand, for example, as a symbol of political power, or songs may be sung in praise of certain officials. In social organizations, social control is widely effectuated through singing songs about the misdeeds of erring individuals usually without mentioning names, but always with identification made certain through indirect reference. Similarly, the wide range of songs for birth, twins, marriage, death, and so forth, fall into this general category. In the field of economics, the use of music in cooperative labor is outstanding. In religion, music frequently serves as a direct means of communication with the gods or spirits, sometimes, for example, through the medium of possession; and musical instruments, as entities, sometimes have symbolic religious meaning. Music may also function as an historic device, as a mean of recounting current events, or of educating children.[5]

Merriam's summation is one in which one can readily see the emphasis on direct functionality of music in African society. A proper understanding of this relationship is absolutely necessary if one is to understand music in the context of African culture. The importance of the role and function of music in pre-colonial African society as a form of communication is further described as follows by Charles Duvelle:

> Music in Africa, perhaps more than elsewhere, is an integral part of life. As a living art, music is religion, work, entertainment; it is associated with gesture and dance; it is closely linked to everyday life in traditional societies. As a means of communication between the visible and invisible worlds, music can play many roles of a semantic kind; since it is very close to spoken language, supporting it or communicating with it, music

---

4. Alan P. Merriam, Notes in the Booklet Africa "South" of the Sahara for the record album of the same title (New York: Folkways Records, 1957), 2.

5. Alan P. Merriam, African Music, Continuity and Change in African Culture, ed. William R. Bascom and Melville J. Herskovits (Chicago: University of Chicago Press, 1959), 72.

becomes a rational and explicit language of its own when expressed through the mouth of a wooden 'talking' drum. It acts as a cement to social institutions; it is the means of identification with a particular group (initiation music, court music, etc.). Without music,many aspects of traditional African life would disappear. [6]

The idea of direct functionality and close integration of music with the rest of the culture,as expressed by Merriam and Duvelle, is perhaps best exemplified in the dance. The importance of the dance in Africa cannot be over-emphasized. Wherever one finds music being made in Africa, one is likely to find dancing occurring simultaneously. The dance in Africa is far more than a choreographic accomplishment; it is an inextricable entity in the entire musical event. The greater significance of the African dance is expressed by A. M. Opoku.

> To us, life with its rhythms and cycles is dance and dance is life. The dance is life expressed in dramatic terms. The most important events in the community have special dances to infuse fuller meaning into the significance of these events. They speak to the mind through the heart. In the European sense, drama is a fact of life on which a spotlight is thrown to remind society of inner conflicts, strengths, and weaknesses, failures and success, hopes and fears as instruments which make us what we are. This is often expressed in the theme of the drama, which is developed into a plot with unravelled actors portraying certain characters to bring the point home. The dance serves a similar purpose in our society and is to us what the conventional theatre is to other racial groups. The dance is a language, a mode of expression springing from the heart, using movements which have their counterparts in our everyday activities to express special and real life experiences, to music or poetic stimulus.[7]

In addition to its role as a vehicle for the drama or the dramatic presentation of life, the dance also serves as a vehicle for the preservation and propagation of the history and customs of African society, and as Opoku points out, a study of the dance will reveal a great deal about African society.

> A study of the dance is therefore a study of our life and soul; and from this we gain deeper insight and comprehension into our ways of living, customs, labour, aspirations, history, geographical and social backgrounds, economic conditions, religious beliefs, moments of joy

---

6. Charles Duvelle, "Oriental Music in Black Africa," <u>African Music</u> (Paris: La Revue Musicale, 1970), 145.

7. A. M. Opoku, "Thoughts From the School of Music and Drama Institute of African Studies," Okyeame, II/I (Legon. Ghana: University of Ghana, 1964), 51.

and sadness; namely our culture. It is a study of the realities that make us the people that we have been and are in the present. [8]

The dancer is likened to any other artist in the society, such as the poet and the composer, the main difference being that the dancer express himself in terms of body movements. The African dance is bound up with elements of the poetic, dramatic, choreographic and musical events. It serves as a vehicle of history, cultural enlightment,and preservations, and must be understood in that light.

The above is offered only as a general overview of the characteristics of traditional African dance. There are countless other parameters which would need to be considered in an in-depth study of the dance, but these are beyond the scope and purpose of this study. These comments are made here for the purpose of showing the relationship between the dance and African society which is one of direct functionality and not just a matter of art for art's sake. In the same way, African-American music uses rhythms, drama,and poetry as vehicles for the depiction of life, and not merely as entertainment and gratification for an elite esoterica.

African music can be shown to be quite varied not only in terms of its many types, functions, dances, instruments and their uses, but also in terms of the many different aspects of scales, melodies, harmonies and rhythms. Africans are known to use pentatonic, hexatonic, and heptatonic scales of indeterminate pitches and intervals. This aspect of African music is extremely important to the later discussion of African retentions. Erich von Hornbostel sees melody evolving from modes which he sees as something strikingly different from scales.[9] He maintains that

> a scale fixes the relative pitch of the notes, and therefore, the intervals, without taking account of their melodic function; a mode, on the contrary, only determines the melodic function of the notes, whereas their relative pitch and the size of the intervals are merely an outcome of that function. [10]

This, then, unlike the western scale, produces a kind of indeterminacy of pitch which provides a much more flexible melodic contour. Hornbostel further contends that non-European melody, which is not conceived harmonically, constitutes a kind of pure melody which is not based on a succession of fixed degrees or scales.[11] Rhythm and harmony also evolve naturally out of pure melody, according to Hornbostel.[12]

---

8.   Ibid.

9.   E. M. von Hornbostel, "African Negro Music," Africa, i/I (1928),

10. Ibid.

11. Ibid., 34.

12. Ibid., 38.

It has been suggested that the simultaneous movement of melodic lines produces so-called "harmony" in African music. For lack of a better term, the word harmony has been used to try to describe these simultaneous sounds. The term is more at home in a European context where fixed scale patterns and a hierarchy of relationships are encompassed by the rules and regulations of tonal, functional harmony. The simultaneous sounds in African music are not so predetermined. A method by which simultaneities are produced is the "spontaneous singing of variants of the melody in combination with the main melody." [13] Another type of "harmony" or simultaneous sound as described by Hornbostel are those that arise as a result of antiphony. [14] This type results from an overlapping of solo and chorus on the first and final notes of a line or tune, When the two meet, the result is what Hornbostel calls a "dichord." Since this "dichord" comes about melodically and not as a result of any harmonic principles, the resulting interval may be of any kind, and may vary from one occurrence to the next. [15] Dichords may occur not only accidentally but also as a result of the chorus being divided into two sections (the same kind of overlapping which occurs when solo and chorus overlap can occur between the two sections of the chorus) and may extend beyond the last note of a tune or phrase or over several of the concluding notes of a phrase (overlapping of melodic lines) and on occasion will extend over the entire last line of a stanza. [16]

Besides the two types of polyphony or "harmony" mentioned above, another type evolves from the use of several musical instruments using scales and intervals of indeterminate pitch. [17] Hornbostel describes this type of simultaneous sound in the following manner:

> Frequently several instruments are played at the same time, or one is played by two men, each using both hands. In this case, two parts move more or less parallel to each other, and also to the vocal melody if there is one. They agree, however, in their melodic outline only, not in the relative size of the intervals. The scale of the instrument in itself mostly precludes an organum in its strict sense; the fourths and fifths are not exact, and, the neighbouring steps are not always equal in size. [18]

---

13. Butcher, Vada E., Development of Materials for a One Year Course in African Music for the General Undergraduate Student. Final Report, (Washington, D. C.: U. S. Department of Health, Education, and Welfare, 1970).

14. von Hornbostel, "African Negro Music," Africa, 1/1 (1928),40.

15. Ibid.

16. Ibid.

17. Ibid.

18. Ibid.

West African Xytophone with gourd resonators

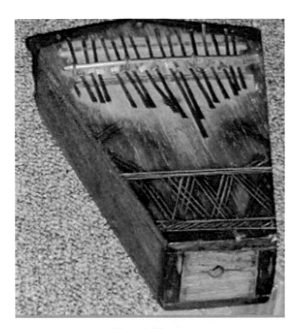

Thumb Piano

Another type of simultaneous sound in African music is described by A. M. Jones as "diody." He characterizes the practice as follows:

Normally, African chorus-singing is diodic, that is, in addition to the song-melody itself, some people are making harmony by singing at what we in the West recognize as consonant intervals, usually, but not **always, below the melody-line. That is the essence of the matter; in** practice both the melody and the harmony line are usually doubled at the octave so as to suit the pitch of both men and women for both parts. Thus the women are singing in harmony and the men are doing the same an octave lower .... (that is , the men are singing the same two pitches an octave lower). As polyphony suggests a distinct discipline belonging to Western music, this seems confusing: we would suggest the term diody,' though 'harmony' seems the easiest word. [19]

From the above description it can be seen that African music does, in fact, contain several types of simultaneous sounds (not necessarily planned or contrived) and that these relationships have been variously described by numerous terminologies, In most cases later in this discussion, the terminology to be used will either be in reference to triadic or tertian sonorities or some type of parallelism.

In addition to the above matter of instruments and their use, scales and harmonies, there is the very complex matter of rhythms in African music. African rhythms are among the most complex in the world. Africans as a rule are not satisfied with one rhythm or meter at any one given time. African rhythmic practices are variously referred to as polymeter, polyrhythm, or cross rhythms. These terms are often used synonymously and interchangeably. In a given ensemble, one may find an entire family of drums consisting of various sizes and timbres. To this may be added a number of other sound-producing instruments such as belts, clappers, rattles, and so on, the entire ensemble numbering in the teens and even much higher. Each player plays a-different rhythmic pattern which he repeats over and over again, or he may improvise on his own pattern, creating an ever changing rhythmic scene.[20] As to how all of these rhythms are combined and executed smoothly, Akin Euba offers the following explanation:

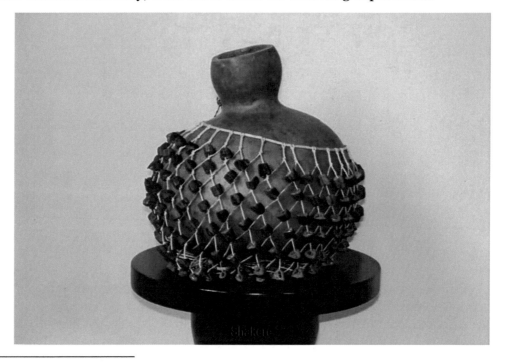

19. A. M. Jones, "The Homogeneity of African Music," <u>Studies In African Music</u> (1959), 216-217.

20. Butcher, <u>Project in African</u> Music, ,80.

Atoke

Talking drum

The truth is that there is always a basic time pattern which is supplied by an easily distinguishable instrument such as a bell or a rattle, or simply by hand clapping. It is against this basic time pattern that all the other instruments will check themselves whenever they suspect somethings may be amiss. [21]

Waterman describes African rhythms as "hot" or "compelling" rhythms.[22] He demonstrates how mixed meters, musical instruments (particularly the drum) and the dance all contribute to the making of hot rhythms. He discusses three aspects of African rhythms which help to describe its "hotness." The quote is a lengthy one and is included here in its entirety because it expresses in a most satisfactory manner the various aspects of African polyrhythms. The third part of the quote deals more with rhythm-making instruments and their use rather than "hot" rhythms.

I

The drum rhythms of African 'hot' music are steady and reliable, although each drum or group of similar drums has, so to speak, its own time signature. This use of what may be called 'mixed metres' is the outstanding trait of African percussion rhythm. The transcriber

---

21. Ibid.

22. Richard A. Waterman, "'Hot' Rhythm In Negro Music," Journal of the American Musicological Society, 1/1 (1948), 24.

trained in the rules of European music, and forced by the conventions of written music to choose some single time signature for his transcription, often finds the problem a considerable one; this may explain why, in many transcriptions of African music, the time-signature is changed every few bars. As the initial major component of 'hot' rhythm, then, we have <u>percussion polyrhythms.</u>

II

Although most African percussion instruments are 'melodic' to the extent that account is taken of their pitch, it has seemed advisable for purposes of discussion to divide African musical rhythms into two categories of percussion and melody. The reason for this lies in the peculiar relationship that exists between the steady and dependable, although complex, beat-patterns of those instruments which figure in the poly-rhythms of the melodies, whether vocal or instrumental. Whereas the accents of European melodies tend to fall either on the thesis or the arsis of the rhythmic foot, the main accents of African melodies—especially those of 'hot' music fall <u>between</u> the down and upbeats. The effect thus produced is that of a temporal displacement of the melodic phrase in its relationship to the percussion phrase to the extent of half a beat.The displacement is usually ahead, so that the melodic anticipates the percussion stroke, although on occasion the percussion accent is allowed to anticipate the melodic beat. The entire rhythmic configuration is always held together, and the displacement is given meaning, by strategically placed melodic accents which coincide with the percussion accents. A second, easily identified trait of African musical rhythm, then, is the 'off-beat phrasing' of melodies.

III

A third characteristic of African music which, while not a trait of the rhythms, nevertheless helps to describe it, concerns the importance accorded to rhythm-making instruments. Almost all African musical instruments are rhythm instruments, The kinds of drums that provide a focus of musical interest for Africans are supplemented by rattles, iron gongs, calabashes, and sticks, all of which contribute to the complexity of African polyrhythms. Trumpets, flutes, and other melodic instruments, on the other hand, are comparatively few. The marimba, the musical bow, and the sansa, which combine rhythmic and melodic functions, give more support to the rhythms of songs with which they are associated than they do to the melodies. Particularly in the 'hot' African music—the music which calls the gods and inspires possession—percussion instruments and their rhythms are heavily emphasized.[23]

---

23. Ibid. 25.

Hot rhythms are also very much a part of African dance, and the dance is an outstanding example of those rhythms. As Richard Waterman explains:

> Every West African youth wishes to excel in dancing, and the dance style of the area may be described most succinctly as a carefully poised response to the rhythms of the drums. The dance of the West African is an essay on the appreciation of musical rhythms. For the performance of a good dancer the, drums furnish the inspiration, in response to which the thread of each rhythmic element contributing to the thunderous whole of the percussion qestalt is followed in movement without separation from its polyrhythmic context. [24]

Percussion instruments and rhythms are ever-present and are of extraordinary importance in the life of the African. These instruments and rhythms are used during farming activities, and while rowing boats down rivers and streams. Drumming is an essential part of religious activities. Often a god will have his own rhythmic pattern which his worshippers will use while invoking him. An African who excels in drumming throughout his life is held in high regard in his community, a fact that underscores the importance of drumming in African communities.[25]

The remarks on the foregoing pages, while in no way claiming any thorough or all-inclusive treatment of African music, have, nevertheless, sufficiently demonstrated that African music often consists of several lines occurring simultaneously (not in the Western sense of polyphony, but as discussed in the previous pages), is highly diverse rhythmically with its many cross rhythms with their polyrhythmic and polymetric subtleties, that it uses highly diverse scalar and melodic materials, and is possessed of not one representative or generalized style but is rather a composite of great stylistic diversity, depending on where it is found in Africa.

---

24. Ibid, 26.

25. Ibid.

India

(Hindi Music)

हिन्दी संगीत

CHAPTER 4

India

The Indian subcontinent is an extensive land mass that is a part of a continent but with considerable geographical independence. The largest and most populous country in that land mass is India, followed by Pakistan, Sri Lanka, Nepal, Bangladesh, Bhutan, and Sikkim. [1] Although these separate countries came about through political and religious strife, the remnants of which still persist today in violent confrontations between Muslims, Sikhs, Hindus, Sinhalese and Tamils, there is much that binds them together, particularly in the realm of music and the arts. [2]

India

1. Funk and Wagnalls, New International Dictionary of the English Language. (Chicago, Illinois: Ferguson Publishing Company, 2001) 1247.

2. Alan Blackwood, Music of the World (Englewood Cliffs, New Jersey: Prentice-Hall, Incorporated, 1991) 64.

Indian culture has existed for over 5000 years, making it one of the oldest cultures in the world. Due to waves of invasions and migrations over thousands of years, it is also one of the most diverse cultures in the world. Ancient Persia, one of the greatest empires of the ancient world, extended from the Nile to Greece and India. This influence can be seen in various chordophones, aerophones, idiophones, and memranophones. Arabic music manifested itself in India in the seventh century due to the movement eastward of Islam. [3]

Indian music is thought to be inherently sacred and is believed to be rooted in the Vedas, the ancient sacred writings of India "It is believed that God himself Is musical sound, the sound that pervades the whole universe, i.e. Nada Brahma" [4]

> *"It is believed that God himself is musical sound, the sound pervades the whole universe, i.e. Nada Brahma. Divine, as is Indian Music, the musician has to cultivate a sense of abandonment, in order to fuse with the Supreme Reality - Nada Brahma. Indian Classical Music derives its essence, not so much from its structure and rules, as from the quest and goal - God."* [5]

Given the central place of the Supreme in Indian belief, it is thought that all other aspects of Indian music are derived from that same source, the Samaveda.

The diagram below shows the evolution of the raga beginning with (nada) the physical vibrations of sound whose connection to the spiritual realm has already been indicated.

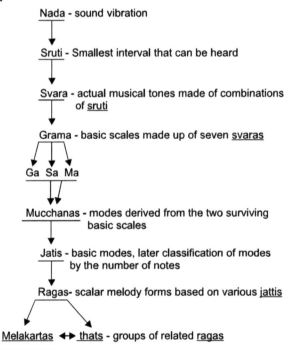

3.   Ibid. 68.

4.   Ruchira Panda, "Indian Classical Music, An Overview."

5.   Ibid. 2.

6.   William Malm, Music Cultures of the Pacific, the Near East, and Asia (Englewood Cliffs, New Jersey: Prentice-Hall, Inc., 1967) 71.

Indian Classical Music is divided into two traditions, the Hindustani tradition of the north and the Carnatic tradition of the south. In both the Hindustani and Carnatic traditions, the raga and the tala are the guiding forces in the unfolding of the music.

The following concepts can be said to govern Indian music. It is:

- Drone-based;

- Raga/Tala oriented;

- Highly improvisatory.

The drone in Indian music is ubiquitous and essential. While it may be made up of what we might call the tonic and dominant, its role is comparable to that of the tonic in western music, that is, a central pillar or home base as the music evolves. It provides a kind of unity in diversity. This is not to say that the music is anything other than melodic, for it does not imply nor is it dependent on the concept of harmony. An Indian performer may have a lifetime affair with a single tonic. Likewise there is no modulation or change of key in a composition, and notes relate to each other simply by their continuity.

The raga in Indian music is somewhat similar to a scale insofar as it contains the notes that may be used. However, it is much more than a simple scale and infinitely more complex. Ragas are also a blueprint, a procedure or a form of melody-making which serves as the basis for creating or improvising. They share characteristics with the Greek modes in terms of their extra-musical characteristics in that they are thought to embody various moods such as happiness, loneliness, tranquility, heroism, and so on. The word means color, mood, or feeling which then becomes a requisite part of the music emanating from a particular raga. Certain ragas are assigned to certain times of the day or night and are associated with certain seasons and occasions. [7]

In addition to their ascending (arohana) and descending (avarohana) forms, they are highly embellished and contain many microtones (shrutis) and other subtleties, which along with their extra-musical considerations makes them rather interesting and complex sources of melodic material. The descending from may be different from the ascending form and may in fact reverse itself momentarily in either. Ragas may have five, six, or seven notes, and even twelve.

The tala is the rhythmic counterpart of the raga It can be viewed a rhythmic mode or metrical cycle upon which the drummer will improvise while melody is being improvised through the raga. There are a certain number of beats in each tala which are repeated continuously throughout the composition. The cycle may be divided into several smaller sections with certain beats being indicated as either

---

7. Ibid, 7.

strong or weak. In a performance an individual might be observed beating tala indicating the cycle and its constituent parts as the progression unfolds.

The third pillar of Indian music is improvisation, wherein the raga and tala are subjected to intense exploration and realization. The central focus of the process is not the procedure itself or the techniques involved, but rather the realization of all that the raga has to offer. This constitutes a profound difference between the raga and the concept of "composition" in Western and Indian music.

> *As Nazir Jairazbhoy characterizes it: "The composition serve as a spring board for these [extemporizations] and a frame of reference to which musicians periodically return. Thus the form is similar to that of the rondo, the compositions alternating with the improvisations." The improvisations themselves are usually made up of previously worked- out phrases, musical elements put together in unique ways for each performance. The intricacy of the structure of these musical elements and the ingenuity of the architectural assembly establish the degree of creativity and inspiration in the performance.* [8]

And now more specifically to the improvisational process itself.

> *Improvisations are not generated on the basis of the composition as such, but are elaborations of the rag. The rag, which has no conceptual analogue in Western music, has been defined by Peter Row "as a set of*

8.   Daniel M. Neuman, The Life of Music in North India (Chicago, Illinois: University of Chicago Press, 1990) 23.

*musical materials that together form a unique modal identity that serves as the basis for composition and improvisation. The significance of the composition then is not in exhibiting itself, but rather in **exhibiting the rag; it is an instance of the rag in both a miniature and** template sense, as microcosm and as generator of authentic versions. This is why the quality of a composition is determined by its success in expressing the essence of a rag and inspiring elaboration of it.* [9]

Improvisation is much more prevalent in the North Indian Hindustani tradition than in the Camatic tradition of the south where "composed" or "fixed" pieces are more common.

Indian Musical Instruments

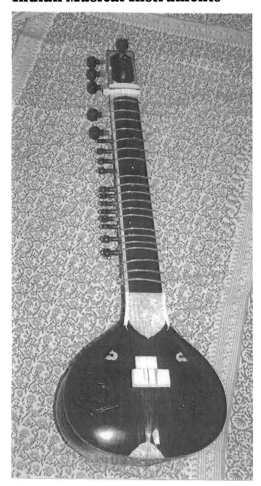

Sitar
(Source: Greg Swanson)

Tampura
(Source: Greg Swanson)

---

9.   Ibid.

Tampura
(Source: Greg Swanson)

Pungi or Bin
(Source: Greg Swanson)

North Indian Tabla
(Source: Greg Swanson)

Harmanium
(Source: Greg Swanson)

DANCE IN INDIA

Dance is also popular in India. It is an interpretive art which is accompanied by gestures and facial expressions along with the dance steps. Mudras (stylized hand gestures) are used creatively as the dance progresses to help express the meaning of the words.

There are two styles of dance in the classical tradition, that of pure dance (nrtta) and expressive dance (nrtya). A performance will usually balance the two types in an individual dance or in a performance of a set of dances. There are at least eight styles of classical dance in India. A few representative types are as follows.

-Kathak

> Embodies Moslem influence. Uses subtle and delicate hand and arm movements along with complex, precise, and powerful foot movements.

-Bharata Natyam

> Very popular in major Indian cities and combines both expressive and pure dance in a complex fabric. It exhibits clear lines and stretched limbs.

-Kathakali

> Uses a complex array of facial expressions, language, gestures, stylized makeup and extremely elaborate costumes.

-Maharis

> Ancient, feminine, magical style danced by temple dancers in the great temples of Orissa. It is endowed with sculptural beauty, pathos, subtlety, and lyricism.

In these and other art forms, an understanding of the concept of rasa is essential in dealing with the fundamentals of aesthetic properties, and central to that understanding is the requisite communication between spectator and performer. The absolute necessity for this is stressed in the <u>Nandikesvara's Abhinayadarpanam.</u> an ancient treatise on dance. [10]

> *"Where the hand goes the eyee follow. Where the eyes go, the mind follows. Where the mind goes, bhava (feeling) follows; and where there is bhava, there rasa (aesthetic fulfillment) arises."*

---

10.   "Indian Dance," <u>Oriental Music Fesival.</u>

Pakistan

(Pakistani Music)

پاکستانی میسک

پاکستانی میسک

پاکستانی میسک

CHAPTER 5

Pakistan

Pakistan is situated in the northwestern part of the Indian subcontinent between Afghanistan and India with Iran on the western border. It also shares borders with Jammu and Kashmir east and southeast and China in the north.

Pakistan

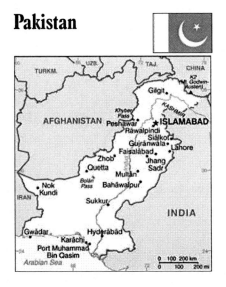

Islam is the leading religion in Pakistan and consequently it is Muslim in culture, but with British and Hindu influences as well. Over 75% of the population of 60,000,000 is rural. Given its location along the Indus River Valley and its history of wars and migrations (conquered by Alexander the Great in the fourth century), Pakistan has many pre-Islamic influences, cultural groups and languages today. Urdu is the national language with other main languages being Pashto, Sindi, Punjabi, and Baluchi. Bengali is also found along with other regional dialects. When British rule ended, and Bangladesh, the former East Pakistan seceded, the Islamic republic of Pakistan was established in 1947. [1]

---

1. "Pakistan." <u>JVC Video Anthology of World Music and Dance</u>. (Montpelier, Vermont: Rounder Records, 1991) 51.

In spite of the strong Islamic influence in Pakistan with its ambivalent and generally negative attitude toward music and dance, classical music traditions closely resembling those of India are able to exist. Both in theory and practice Pakistani music is essentially the same as the Hindustani tradition of North India The characteristic drum of North India, the tabla is used along with other typically North Indian chordophones such as the sitar, tampura, sarangi, sarod and a flute called the bansuri. Persian influence is evidenced by the santur, a Middle Eastern dulcimer. The harmonium, a portable reed organ from Europe is extremely popular in North India and Pakistan.[2]

In addition to the chordophones listed above, these membranophones are found.

- *dholak*	Cylindrical, double-headed drum used for dancing and singing.
-*dhol*	Larger and similar to the dholak. An outdoor drum played with sticks.
-*damru*	Hour-glass shaped, double-headed drum struck by knotted cords and played principally by nomadic entertainers.
-*naqqara*	Kettle drums of clay or metal on which two curved beaters are used.
-*duff*	A frame drum from the Middle East, sometimes with with tambourine-like discs played with the hand to accompany women's songs.

The following chordophones are used.

-*ghungru*	Ankle bells.
-*dando*	Short wooden stick.
-*manjira*	Hand cymbals made of brass.
-*chimta*	Metal tongs with brass discs.
-*matka*	Large clay waterpot.

Aerophones exist as both flute and oboe types

-*shanai*	A double-reed instrument used outdoors.
-*bin*	A bagpipe-like instrument used for snake charming.
-*chang*	A jaw's harp of metal a bamboo.
-alghoza	A wooden double apple flute.
-*nar*	End-blown flute.

---

2.   JVC Anthology. 52.

Given the proximity of Iran and other parts of the Middle East and Afghanistan and India to Pakistan, it is not surprising that these cultures share a considerable number and variety of instruments.[3]

The Subcontinent Beyond India and Pakistan

Bangladesh, Nepal, Bhutan, Sikkim, *Sri* LanKa

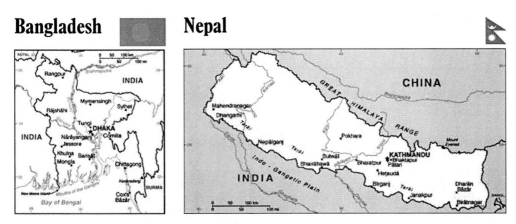

Bangladesh   ## Nepal

Formally <u>Bangladesh</u> was East Pakistan which until 1955 was known as East Bengal. It gained its independence in 1971. Given its history and location, it is historically and culturally akin to the old Indian province of Bengal. This can be seen in a number of genres that have been retained.

-Rabindra-sangeet

A song and dance genre.

-Kirtan

Devotional songs based on a collection of Hindu poetry *(Vaisnava padavali)*.

-Baul songs

A mystical sect in 'which beggars sing songs while sometimes dancing and playing drums.

-Bhatiali and Sari

Boatmen's songs, the former being slow while the latter are more indicative of faster moving waters or perhaps races. [4]

---

3. Regula Qureshi, "Pakistan," <u>New Grove's Dictionary of Music and Musicians</u>, 20 vols., ed. Stanley Sadie (London: Macmillan, 1980), 106-108.

4. Blackwood, <u>Music of the World.</u> 73-74.

Bhutan

Nepal, situated contiguously with Bhutan and Sikkim, links it to India and Tibet. The links can be observed in the following genres.

-Minstrel musicians

> Patterned after the Indian caste system, that is, their songs, dances, and instruments are identified by groups distinction.

—damyan

> A long-necked lute probably from Afghanistan.

-manirimdu

> Ritual dances closely connected to Tibet, perhaps to their monastery dance dramas. They are performed by the Nepalese Sherpas (mountain-climbers) who are ethnically akin to Mongolians and Tibetans.[5]

Although tied culturally and historically to mainland India, Sri Lanka features its own culture which is influenced much more by Buddhism than Hinduism. Both prehistoric and indigenous musical examples can be found.

-Vedda songs

> Songs created by the Vedda or Yakkha people close to prehistoric times. The Vedda are thought to be descended from an early Indo-Autstraloid group.

5.   Blackwood, Music of the World, 74.

-Sinhalese music (Sinhala - resplendent land, Ceylon, Taprobane) Primarily dance music accompanied mainly by drums but also with ankle bracelets, bells, and hand cymbals. Costumes and masks hearkening back to prehistoric times (Yakkha) are still in use. Dance steps are learned through the use of mnemonics.

—Hindu dance routines

Hindu myths and legends are acted out. Peacocks, elephants, and monkeys are represented in stylized fashion.

-Kandyan dance

Named after Kandy the ancient royal capital. Groups of dancers of five to six each dance while accompanying themselves on percussion instruments including cymbals and drums.[6]

Sri Lanka

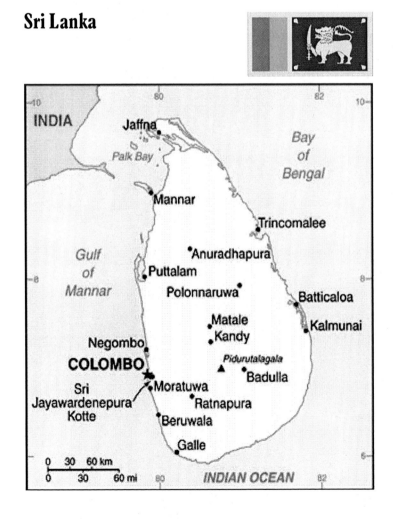

6.   Ibid.

China

(Chinese Music)

華人音樂

CHAPTER 6

China

China

China is the second largest and most populated country in East Asia and the world with nearly a billion people. Since 1949 China has been divided into the People's Republic of China with its capital in Bejing and the Republic of China on the island of Taiwan with its capital in Taipei. China shares borders with the Indian Subcontinent, Pakistan, Russia, Mongolia, Korea, and Southeast Asia. Our consideration of Chinese music will begin beyond prehistoric times beginning with the Shang dynasty (1523 - 1027 B.C.), this because it is the first dynasty documented in Chinese history. Even more importantly for our purposes is the dynasty that followed, namely, the Chou dynasty (c. 1027 -256 B.C.)in which Confucius lived, and to which so much of ancient Chinese philosophy, education, and general thinking is attributed. [1]

---

1. William H. Harris and Judith S. Levey, eds., The New Columbia Encyclopedia. (New York: Columbia University Press, 1975) 535-536.

The proper order of things was deeply imbedded in the Confucian way of life, and he believed that music was an essential part of the quest for conformity and discipline. Confucius therefore proffered the notion found in The Book of Change that "there is nothing better than music in reforming people's manners and customs." Confucius further believed that there were essentially two kinds of music, namely, "proper" and "extravagant." Proper music was believed to influence human behavior in positive ways while extravagant music was thought to be deleterious. Proper music was "ritual music played in unison with long, broad rhythms, slow tempos and simple melodies." Extravagant music on the other hand was characterized as "loud, and fast" with its attendant negative effects. So important was music during the Chou dynasty that a Minister of Music was appointed to insure its proper place.[2]

The disciplined, proportioned aspects of Chinese music championed by Confucius derived from mathematical implications. And in fact, the twelve lus, the twelve chromatic semitones of the octave, are said to be derived mathematically. The story goes that the inventor of the lus (or laws), Huang Ti, sent Ling Lun, Minister of Music, to find bamboo tubes to make the lus.[3] Whether or not Ling Lun actually cut the tubes to the precise measurements needed to produce or match pitches already in use is anyone's guess. A reasonable assumption could be that a gradual understanding and articulation of what happens naturally in the overtone series evolved over time and came to be accepted and offered as an explanation, as echoed by Pythagoras and others. An interesting account of how the division of the tubes might have taken place is offered as follows.

Now, what led the inventor to the division of the octave into twelve semitones, each represented by one *lu* ? Several versions are given :—

1°. *Some say that he arrived at it by listening to the singing of the Pengs or Fengs (a powerful tribe living south of the Yangtze-kiang), the voices of the men giving him six semitones and those of the women the remaining six.*

2°. *Others give the same theory with this particular change, that the Fengs were not human beings, but birds; the male being called (feng), and the female (huang). Unfortunately for this theory, a third account assures us that these birds were simply imaginary.*

3°. *Another writer attributes to the rolling waves of the Yellow River the idea of the first sound. The bamboos growing on its borders were used to render it.*

4°. *Another writer, less poetical but not less positive, is convinced that Ling Lun cut his bamboos according to the terms of a triple progression of 12 numbers, as 1. 3, 9. 27, 81, etc., which, indeed, exhibit the numerical values of a series of perfect fifths.*[4]

---

2. Bruno Nettl, Charles Capwell, Philip V. Bohlman, Isabel K. Wong, and Thomas Turino, Excursion in World Music. (Englewood Cliffs, New Jersey: Prentice Hall, 1992), 90.

3. J. A. Van Aalst, Chinese Music, (New York, New York: Paragon Book Reprint Corporation, 1966) 6.

4. Van Aalst, Chinese Music, 7.

It must be pointed out that the twelve perfect fifths that make up the lus will not sound exactly like the twelve semitones of the Western octave. The reason for this is that these perfect fifths combined are greater than the the 2 to 1 ratio of of the octave. This small difference is called the ditonic comma (Pythagoras) and can be expressed by the ratio 531,441 to 524,288. This may seem minute, but to ears accustomed to Western tempered music, the difference can be challenging. It may at first sound harsh, or too flat or too sharp, or just generally out of tune.[5]

Chinese music and the language are closely connected due to the fact that Chinese is a tonal or inflected language. Words must be spoken at the right pitch in order to insure the desired meaning. Consequently, it may be difficult to know where speaking ends and song begins, and vice versa.

Chinese music is essentially non-harmonic and focuses principally on melodic development. However, Western theory and harmony have made significant inroads and is now quite common.

As far as scalar resources go, pentatonicism rules, although in modern times, two additional semi-tones have been added to the pentatonic scale bringing it closer to the heptatonic scale of Western music.

In previous times Chinese instruments were classified into eight categories corresponding to eight natural materials found on earth, such as, bamboo, gourd, clay, wood, metal, skin, stone, and reed. This classification is discussed in Chapter 1 under Organology. Today the categories of percussion, wind, and string are not uncommon.

The following are a few representative instruments classified according to the old and the new categories. (p.58)

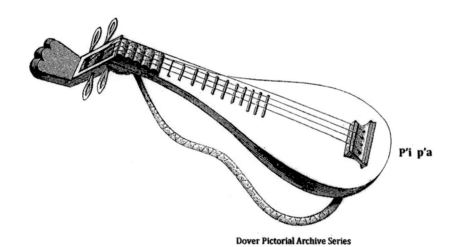

P'i p'a

Dover Pictorial Archive Series

---

5.   Van Aalst, Chinese Music, 8.

Cheng

Ti-tzu

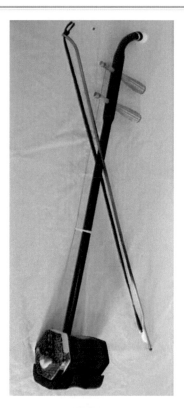

Er-hu

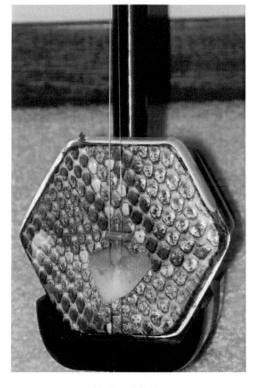

Body of Er-hu

	Descriprion	Old Classification	New Classification
Chin	Plucked zither, seven strings, four feet long.	Silk	String
Pipa	Gourd-shaped, four strings, frets.	Silk	String
Sheng	Several bamboo tubes Each with a reed protruding from a tea pot-shaped gourd with a sound resembling a small reed organ.	Bamboo/Gourd	Wind
Cheng	Plucked zither with sixteen strings.	Silk	String
Hsiao	Bamboo flute with six fingerholes, end-blown.	Bamboo	Wind
Ti	Bamboo flute, side-blown, seven holes.	Bamboo	Wind
Pang-ku	Small drum on a pedestal.	Skin	Percussion
Yun-lo	Suspended bronze gongs.	Metal	Percussion
Yu	A crouched tiger with saw-like projections which are struck.	Wood.	Percussion
Hsuan	A globular flute made of clay with up to seven fingerholes.	Ciav/Earth	Wind
Pien-ch'ing	Lithophone with 16 stone slabs struck with hammers, each rendering a different Ditch.		Percussion

Sona

Ruan
Moon Lute

Gu
Barrel Drum

A Contemporary View
(An interview with Mr. Tian)

Mr. Tian, what is your profession or vocation?

I am a choir conductor and singer. I teach at a music school and I teach professional groups.

What instrument(s) do you play?

Piano.

Are there distinctions between professional, amateur, or folk musicians in the culture, and how are such distinctions played out?

Yes. Non-professional music would be amateur or folk music and is associated with daily life. In the 19th century there was an emphasis on diversity, but it is now recognized that due to Westernization, there is a need to preserve traditional music, so much so that folk music is funded.

How much Westernization is there?

There is some, but 70 - 80% of the music is Chinese.

How is music defined in the culture. Is there a word that covers all music or is there different terminology for different types of music?

Music is organized rhythms used to express emotions. As Schumann said, "Music is the end of language. " Music expresses emotions and consists of rhythm, language (melody, harmony, etc.), monophony and also polyphony. Although heterophony exists, there is no technical term for it. There is different terminology for different types of musics.

What is the purpose of music in the culture?

To make people happy, but also to express emotions, good, bad, whatever emotion is involved.

Is there a distinction between good and bad music?

Yes. Good music should express true emotions and should be harmonious, that is, it should bring harmony out of chaos. Confucianism still manifests itself in the traditional music of China today.

What categories of music exist today?

- *Folk Songs.*

- *Quyi, a genre combining talking and singing, a kind of regional operatic story-telling performed by small groups in tea houses, usually involving a singer and a pipa or erhu.*

- *Singing and Dancing.*

- *Opera*

  <u>Regional Forms</u>

  a) *Bejing*

  b) *Sichaun*

  c) *Huangmei (Anhui Province)*

  d) *Chu Opera (Hubei)*

  e) *Han Opera*

  f) *Instrumental Music*

How does music change from one region to the next? *By dialect, culture and custom.*

How is music composed and/or preserved?

It is composed to express emotions, and is preserved in score, on tape and CD.

What is the relationship between music and politics?

Political control is less nowadays and music is no longer a propaganda tool. Composers are free to express themselves as they wish. Christian, Gospel Music and Western holiday music is played and allowed.

Are there prescribed gender roles in musical perfonnances or other activities?

Anyone can perform anywhere, anytime, and play any instrument they wish.

What is the relationship between music and language?

The tonal aspects of Chinese language are manifested in vocal music. the score must match the words and must be cognizant of four tones and the proper placement of them, otherwise the wrong meaning is conveyed. Language affects the expressions in music. Music is a common language among people in the world.

How has music changed as a result of modernization, Westernization, syncretism, Political changes, and so on?

All of these factors are reflected in changes that have and are taking place today.

How does one properly approach aesthetic considerations and evaluative judgments In Chinese music.

Through training and talent.

Can you comment on a few instruments and their place and function?

*Yes. First the **erhu**. This instrument expresses the essence of Chinese music. It can play solo or in ensembles. I like the Western violin because it is close to the **erhu**. The piano because of its fixed pitches, can limit the ability to express emotions.*

*The **Zhu** Di (bamboo flute) comes in different lengths and keys. It is used for many different functions and not confined to any one.*

*The **sona** (double-reed aerophone or oboe) depicts very strong emotions and is used for weddings and funerals.*

*The **sheng** and the organ operate on the same principle.*

What is the most popular music today?

It includes symphonic music, folk songs, popular music, and Broadway Musicals. Even rap and hip-hop are enjoyed by the young people.

Chinese Opera

Western and Chinese opera share some characteristics, but otherwise there are striking differences. Both can be said to be the consummate synthesis of dramatic and musical elements including speaking, singing, acting, dancing, staging, choreography and the like. The differences will be seen in how these various components are employed. The types of regional operas have been listed in the previous Tian conversation while this discussion centers mainly around Bejing Opera.

While Western opera is often accompanied by sizeable instrumental ensembles, such accompaniment in Bejing Opera, like other elements in the genre, is rather economical. The *Hu chin,* an instrument with two silk strings and played with a horsehair bow is commonly used. A moon-shaped guitar with four strings called the *Yueh chin,* along with the *P'iP'a (melon-shaped lute)* and the *Titzu* (bamboo flute) are often used. Percussion instruments (drums, clackers, gongs, cymbals) are extremely important in Chinese opera. They are not just for background sounds, but are an integral part of the drama as it unfolds. Nearly every occurrence, movements, gestures, and vocal utterances, are accompanied by some kind of percussion stroke. Such strokes are particularly effective in scenes involving pantomime and acrobatics where every movement and gesture are highlighted.

Scenery is less elaborate in Chinese opera, and in fact is minimal. The characters have very little if any assistance from scenery or props. In the absence of such, movements and gestures take on an essential role, not unlike the stock characters and codification that permeate the genre in general. Costumes on the other hand are quite numerous and feature enormous variety and bright colors. There is a kind of type casting wherein categories of dress are designated, such as, for scholars, rulers, scholars, and so on. Colors are also used to indicate so many aspects of the drama, such as personal status, character, rank, and the particular role being played. Colorful costumes are unique to both Western and Chinese opera, but the heavily-painted faces are more typical of Chinese opera.

Stylization is another feature that distinguishes the two types of opera. This conformity to a designated style (slow, deliberate, exaggerated, intense) rather than to what might be considered a more natural style, can be both inviting or repelling, depending on one's familiarity with such stylization. Westerners are sometimes startled and confused by the vocal styles and choreography emanating from such stylistic practices.

Bejing Opera is recognized as a National Drama because it is a genuine Chinese art that emphasizes the virtues of justice, righteousness, chastity, loyalty, and filial piety. No doubt this is but another manifestation of Confucianism which still runs deep in Chinese culture today. [6]

---

6.   Anonymous. "Chinese Music," (Taipei, Taiwan: China Publishing Co., 1977) 1.

CHAPTER 7

Tibet

Tibet

Tibet is located in the southwest corner of China, tucked away in the Himalayan Mountains. There Buddhism that had entered from India flourished until the Chinese invasion in 1950. When the invasion took place, the Dalai Lama, spiritual and temporal leader of Tibet, and less than a hundred Buddhist monks were able to escape. They have regrouped in India, and although some few have been allowed to return, many are still in exile in India and elsewhere.

An indigenous religion called *bon* existed alongside of Buddhism when it entered Tibet in the 7th century and still survives today albeit under the careful eye of the Chinese government as does Tibetan Buddhism.[1] Some Tibetan Buddhist monks practice Tantric Buddhism, an advanced meditational system, which like other Buddhist sects has at its core a kind of chant style that is done on a very low pitch- They practice a kind of harmonic or overtone chant, whereby they are able to cause certain tones in the overtone series to surface which are normally too subtle to be heard, thereby enabling each monk to sing a three note chord. The technique defies ordinary principles of physiology and takes years of training and discipline to accomplish. It is thought that the technique might have come from

---

Mongolian *xoomij* singing. The only other known source of this style is among certain Russian groups, particularly those of the Tuva region.

When engaging in these multiphonic chants, the Tibetan Buddhists do not see themselves as performers, but rather as practitioners of the faith. They see their work as an offering and as part of the quest for enlightenment.

> *In Tibet, these seemingly non-melodic chants not only are intended to communicate with the Buddha and his followers but to offer the performer a possible path out of the objective world toward inner transformation and eventual enlightenment. The challenging low pitch and the frequent clouding of the sung text with extra syllables serves as protection for these goals. The proper and safe use of such ritual material must be limited, in the Tibetan view, to those who truly understand its meaning and its power.* [2]

Musical instruments may be found in Tibetan Buddhist rituals as well. Some of the most common are:

-dril-bu	-	handbell
-rol-mo	-	cymbals
-gandi	-	wooden board that signals time of day
-chos-rnga	-	large tacked barrel drum mounted on a pole and played with a curved stick
-lag-rnga	-	a smaller portable version of the *chos-rnga*
-damaru	-	small hourglass-shaped drum
-thod-dam	-	a drum made of the tops of two human skulls with beaters attached
-rag-dung	-	large telescoping trumpets made of copper
-rgya-gling	-	a *zurna*, a double-reed aerophone used to play preludes and interludes to chants[3]

Although ritual music dominated in the theocratic setting of Buddhist Tibet, there was and is a folk and art music tradition in as well. Folk songs deal with daily life and include work songs, love songs, and nomadic or pastoral songs. Long epic songs dealing with mythic heroes. *Nangma* and *toshe* are forms of art music which in recent times have fused with popular pentatonic songs, Western pop, and Indian film music. Although Chinese pentatonicism still manifests itself, six and seven-tone scales may also be found. [4]

---

2. William P. Malm, <u>Music Cultures of the Pacific, the Near East, and Asia.</u> (Upper Saddle River, New Jersey: Prentice-Hall, Inc., 1996) 168-169.
3. Ibid, 169-170
4. Alves. <u>Music of the Peoples of the World,</u> 115,118

Japan

(Japanese Music)

日本の音楽

CHAPTER 8

Japan

Japan

Japan is made up of a number of islands. The four main islands are Hokkaido, Honshu, Kyushu, and Shikoku. A number of smaller islands are also a part of Japanese territory. Of the Rukyu group, Okinawa is the largest. It's as returned to Japan in 1972 after having been captured by the United States during World War II. Japan is a densely populated country with a population of over 104 million. Tokyo is the capital of Japan and Shintoism and Buddhism are the main religions.

Chinese influence runs deep in Japanese culture, that being attributable not only to the coming of Buddhism from China in the 6th century, but particularly to the influence of Confucianism on Japanese thought and development.[1] Chinese influence on Japanese music is clear and unmistakable as will be pointed out in the discussion that follows. Pentatonicism is imbedded in both Chinese and Japanese music but with a distinct difference and flavor. The Chinese pentatonic is anhemitonic, that is, without half-steps. It can be approximated on the Western piano by playing the black keys. The difference in tuning between the piano and the Chinese system as discussed in Chapter 5 allow for only an approximation. The Japanese pentatonic on the other hand is hemitonic (uses half-steps] giving the music a flavor that is immediately distinguishable from Chinese music.

On the one hand, Japan is tradition-bound, no doubt due to its location which kept it out of the path of invasion and for a long while away from external influence. On the other hand, Japan became open to foreign influence, and its ancient musical traditions began to be altered by China, Korea, and even India. [2] We can learn much about Japanese musical traditions by focusing on four genres, namely, **Noh, Kabuki, Gagaku,** and **Bunraku.**

The Noh drama would be comparable to Grand Opera or Opera Seria in the West, in that it would not necessarily be accessible to those who are unfamiliar with the participating parameters and their meanings. As William Malm points out,

> *Noh is a study in literature, theatre, aesthetics, and a type of gesamkunstwerk, It must be understood that Noh, more than Western opera, is a gestalt of equally contributing arts, non of which can honestly be said to be more important than the others.*[3]

The meaning of the word Noh which is "accomplishment," is further evidenced by Malm.

> *Growing out of a host of early theatricals, noh found a means of uniting the arts of music, dance, drama, and decor in such a way as to retain the best elements of its predecessors while deleting their mutual inconsistencies when combined in the noh theatre. This was done by building each play on a central evocative theme, creating poetry in keeping with this mood, and maintaining and developing this idea by means of all the other dramatic arts. Each art was held in check so that the reality of the theme would not be destroyed by the intrusion of the reality of the component arts. In noh, the balance between*

1.   William H. Harris and Judith S. Levey, eds., The New Columbia Encyclopedia. (New York: Columbia University Press, 1975) 9.

2.   Oriental Music Festival. (Elvet Hill, Durham, England: School of Oriental Studies, 1982).

3.   William P. Malm, Japanese Music and Musical Instruments. (Rutland, Vermont: Charles E. Turtle Company, 1973) 105.

highly refined abstraction and the dramatic necessity of human emotions is one of the most delicate and perhaps most successful attempts in world drama.[4]

This accomplishment then is the heart and soul of Noh which will now be coupled with the attendant music and instruments.

Voices playing various roles do so by utilizing the technique of stylization. The flute and drum ensemble that accompanies the Noh drama is called the *hayashi*. It consists of *nohkan,* a transverse bamboo flute with seven holes. The drums of the hayashi are the *ko-tsuzumi, o-tsuzumi,* and the *taiko.* The first two are hour-glass shaped drums with the ko-tsuzumi being larger than the o-tsuzumi. These drums, like the nohkan are lacquered and very colorful and ornate. The third drum is the *taiko,* which is barrel-shaped drum that sits on a pedestal.[5]

The drums of the hyashi weave a fabric that is both complex and intriguing. As William Alves describes it:

> *Noh drumming consists of certain standard patterns strung together and varied by each drummer. Different drummers may play different patterns at the same time, not necessarily synchronized, and this layered effect is one of the distinctive characteristics of Noh. Nevertheless, the drummers are listening to one another. If anything, the freedom of the rhythm necessitates even closer attention than in more pulsatile music.* [6]

Malm underscores the complexity of the drumming techniques.

> *There is also the problem of the exact relation of these patterns to each specific situation. This can be learned only by experience. It is the guarded secret of teachers who inculcate this esoteric knowledge by a slow rote method. An added problem is that each guild interprets these patterns in a slightly different way. This makes it difficult and sometimes impossible for certain drummers to perform together. If a student learns a certain school of ko-tsuzumi, then he is automatically committed to learning other special schools of o-tsuzumi, taiko, and flute in order to coordinate his knowledge. When musicians of various clans perform together, they must meet before the performance and decide whose version of each play they are going to use. Occasionally this is not done and there are unfortunate discrepancies between the parts.* [7]

---

4. Ibid.131.

5. William Alves, <u>Music of the Peoples of the World.</u> (Belmont, California: Thomson-Schirmer, 2006), 211.

6. Ibid.. 212.

7. William Malm, <u>Japanese Music and Musical Instruments.</u> 126.

Tsuzumi

Dover Pictorial Archive Series

This classical Japanese theater is characterized by stylization, a high degree of refinement, and typical Japanese reserve. The slow, stylized movements of the actors suggest a kind weightlessness and timelessness which is very unlike Western theater. It has come a long way from the comedy, pantomime, and acrobatics of the folk plays in which it is rooted, but then evolved into a sophisticated genre for the ruling class, and has most recently continued that evolution to become an attraction for the middle class and other interested artistic seekers.[8]

Another form of theater called Kabuki developed after Noh. While Noh was a thing of the upper imperial classes, Kabuki appealed to the middle-class and the common folk. It is said that Kabuki was invented by a female temple dancer named Okuni who upon leaving the temple went to Kyoto and began performing dances there. In time these dances grew and took the form of plays and became known as Kabuki in the sixteenth century. Eroticism and cross-gender roles were common in Kabuki which on occasion prompted government intervention.

Today female roles are played largely by *onnagata* (female impersonators) who are highly respected and talented. Another feature, that of realism, no doubt in some measure accounts for its widespread popularity in contradistinction to the rather esoteric appeal of Noh and Gagaku.[9]

The musical ensembles used in Kabuki were borrowed pretty much borrowed intact from other genres such as Bunraku, Noh, and others. The four standard ensembles are the Geza, **Debayashi, Shitakata,** and the **Gidayu.** They are

8.   William Alves. Music of the Peoples of the World, 210.

9   James P. O'Brien, Non-Western Music and the Western Listener. (Dubuque, Iowa: Kendall/ Hunt Publishing Co., 1977) 72.

constituted and function as follows.

Geza

- -offstage group
- -four players
- -nohkan, shamisen, percussion
- -sound effects

Debayashi

- -onstage group
- -core ensemble of Kabuki
- - four to eight shamisens and male chorus

O-Daiko
(Double-headed Barrel Drum)

Shitakata

- onstage in front of debayashi on lower platform

- nohkan and sometimes takebue and shinobue (flutes), ko-tsuzumi, o-tsuzumi, and taiko (drums), and debayashi singers

Gidayu

-narrator

-onstage or offstage

-voice and shamisen or three or four of each

-a pair called *chobo*[10]

Another important feature of Kabuki is *Nagauta,* meaning "long song", which refers to the lyric material found therein and also refers generally to the lyric genre of shamisen music. The sound of Naguata is unique and very non-Western. William Malm describes it as follows.

The tone is said to originate in the abdomen, and as it rises passes from a primarily chest tone to more of a head tone. The throat remains very tense and the tone is forced into the upper register without resorting to falsetto. In the twentieth century, the Kenseikai school of nagauta under Kineya Kisaburo began to use falsetto (uragoe) in the style of the softer kiyomoto and shinnai musics.

---

10. William Alves. Music of the Peoples of the World. 213.

This method nearly overwhelmed the classical vocal style but of late there has been a tendency to return to the traditional manner. One reason for the continued existence of this more difficult and, at times, painful method, is that it creates a much stronger and more intense sound.[11]

The style definitely requires some adjustment on the part of the listener who might encounter it from an etic point of view. However, once one recognizes and perchance accepts the obvious differences between this style and the Western style of vocal production, one is then transported to another dimension with enhanced auditory sensibilities.

Historically there have been two types of Kabuki plays. One is called *jidaimono* which deals with "pseudo-historical period pieces." The other is called *sewamono* which features "stories dealing with plebian life of the Edo period". These ancient types have given way to modern plays in recent times.[12]

11. William P. Malm, Nagauta. (Westpoint, Connecticut: Greenwood Press, Publishers, 1973) 49-50.

12. William P. Malm, "Japan," New Grove's Dictionary of Music and Musicians. 522.

Perhaps even more rigid and esoteric than Noh theatre is the genre of Gagaku. This is the imperial court music of Japan. Gagaku is a manifestation of Korean importation as well as music from China. This is seen in two types of gagaku, namely, *komagaku*, "music of the right" from Korea, and *togaku*, "music of the left" from China and India.[13] If the music is purely instrumental, it is called *kangen*. If it used as an accompaniment to dancing, it is called *bugaku*. In fact this music is heard exclusively in Japan and not in the land of its origin. [14]

Gagaku is mystifying to the Western observer, due to its highly stylized character. Dance steps are extremely slow, almost seemingly imperceptible at times. Likewise the singing and dance steps are very deliberate and filled with intensity. Elaborate robes and masks are worn by the performers with symbolic colors and characterizations of the dances and moods inherent therein. [15]

There are four categories of music in Gagaku. Two of them have already been mentioned and are now reiterated here with further explanation. Kangen, or instrumental music, is played by wind and string instruments. Bukagu, or

13. William P. Malm, <u>Japanese Music and Musical Instruments.</u> 89.

14. <u>Oriental Musical Festival.</u>

15. James P. O'Brien, <u>Non-Western Music and the Western Listener.</u> 71.

dance music, will use essentially the same instruments with the exception of an additional zither and lute found in Kangen. The other two types are songs and Shinto ritual music, the latter being distinguished by its use for religious purposes. The following is an outline of instruments used in all four categories of Gagaku.

Aerophones

-Ryuteki	flute, bamboo.transverse, seven holes
-Komabue	flute, transverse, short and thin, six holes
-Hichiriki	small oboe, bamboo, nine fingerholes
-Sho	mouth organ, seventeen bamboo tubes each containing a reed and inserted in a wind chest

Chordophones

-Biwa	lute, flatback, four silk strings
-So	ong zither, six feet, plucked, thirteen silk strings

Idiophone

-Shoko	bronze gong, round, in frame with stand

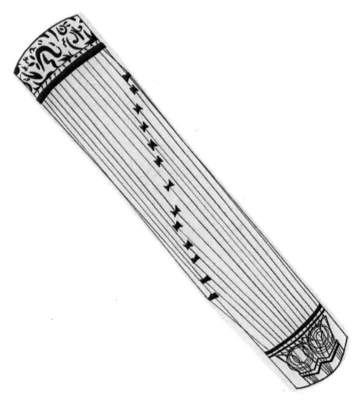

Koto

Memhranophones

  -Kakko two-headed barrel drum on a stand

  -San No
  Tsuzumi large, hour-glass shaped with two heads

  -Taiko two-headed large flat drum suspended from a frame and
       on a stand [16]

Gagaku, being the property of the imperial households and preserved in the palace, was never accessible to the common folk who were not associated with the imperial courts. Even today it is essentially a museum relic which nevertheless remains important as a unique aspect of Japanese history and culture.

The fourth genre to be discussed is **Bunraku,** the puppet theater of Japan. Bunraku features some of the most unique puppets in the world. The puppets are life-size and are manipulated by puppeteers who are often covered from head to toe in white or black except for the senior puppeteer whose face may remain uncovered. As many as three puppeteers may be employed to manipulate various parts of the puppet including its eyebrows, making them extremely life-like. There is a single storyteller *[tayu),* often a virtuoso singer who provides emotive narration to the accompaniment of a shamisen.[17] The *tayu* and the shamisen player seek to bring life and emotional vitality to the puppets, sometimes subtly and at times forcefully and in an exaggerated manner.

> *The whole point of bunraku is to portray human emotions and situations of life so that people's hearts are moved, so that they feel something special about the particular aspect of life the play deals with, whether loyalty, sacrifice, one of the many forms of love, or a dilemma one encounters in life.*[18]

The tayu uses a vocal style called *gidayubushi* which was developed in Osaka by Takemoto Gidayu. It consists of lyrical songs, heightened speech and chants. The shamisen which accompanies this style provides preludes, postludes, and interludes while employing sterotyped patterns in different versions.[19]

16. Shigeo Kishibe, record jacket notes for Traditional Music of Japan. (Victor Records JL-32-4).

17. Oriental Music Festival.

18. Linda Fujie, "East Asia/Japan," Worlds of Music: An Introduction to the Music of the World's Peoples. 4th ed., Jeff Todd Titon, ed., (Belmont, CA: Schirmer-Thomson, 2002) 354.

19. Isabel Wong, 'The Music of Japan," Excursions in World Music. Bruno Nettl, et al., (Upper Saddle River, NJ, 2008) 143.

Shamisen

Dover Pictorial Archive Series

Bunraku has flourished in Japan since the Edo period (1615-1868). This period is also known as the Tokugawa period because of the control of the Tokugawa clan under whom the government was moved to Edo which is called Tokyo today. The rise of the merchant class and the attendant city life in Osaka, a major business town, provided audiences for such theatrical performances. [20]

Today, Japan is among the most industrialized nations in the world and is probably the most westernized nation in East Asia. In high-tech industries and economically in general, Japan has far surpassed other parts of the modernized world. Automobiles, computers, and even the Western piano have become a substantial part of their burgeoning economy and global influence. However, in spite of its rather prominent place in the global village, westernization and modernization have not obliterated the rich cultural heritage of Japan, particularly in their musical and theatrical genres.

---

20. William P. Malm, <u>Music Cultures of the Pacific, the Near East, and Asia,</u> (Upper Saddle River, New Jersey: Prentice-Hall, Inc., 1996) 239.

Korea

(Korean Music)

한국음악

CHAPTER 9

Korea

Korea, North

Korea, South

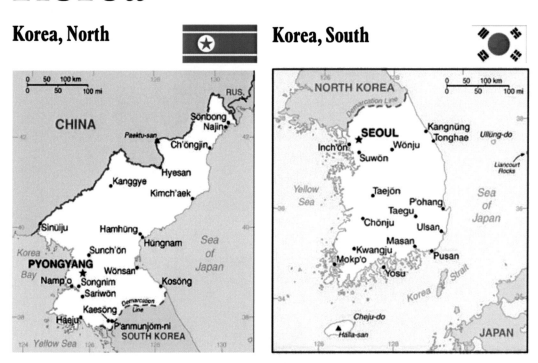

Korea is situated on a peninsula in eastern Asia roughly between mainland China and Japan. The Yellow Sea is to the west while the Sea of Japan is to the east. To the north, Korea shares borders with China and Japan. Buddhism and Confucianism are the main religions, however, the latter is viewed more today as a mere ethical system rather than religious one. An influential indigenous religion is one called Chon-do-gyo, which is a syncretic blend of Taoism, Confucianism, and Buddhism.

Although it is known that the Koreans descended from a tribal people known as the Tungus or Tunguzic, a Siberian ethnic group, their documented history begins with Chinese involvement in the 12th century B.C. with the founding of a colony at Pyongyang by a Chinese scholar named Ki-tze. Chinese influence reigned for centuries following until the coming of Mongol rule in the 13th century. Chinese dominance returned until the coming of the Manchu invasions in the 17th century. Next came Japanese influence which resulted in the annexation of Korea to Japan. At the end of World War II Korea was divided and in 1948 the two republics of North and South Korea were established. Pyongyang is the capital of North Korea and Seoul the capital of South Korea. North Korea maintained a close relationship with the then Soviet Union and with Communist China. After the Korean War, precipitated by an attack on South Korea by North Korea, attempts were made to effect peaceful reunification which never materialized. Hostilities remain between North Korea and the United States while South Korea has looked principally to the United States for foreign aid.[1]

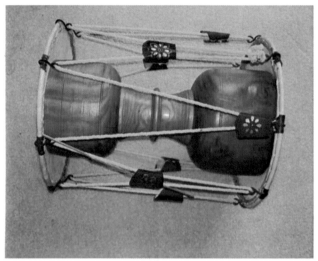

Chang-gu
(Large Deum)

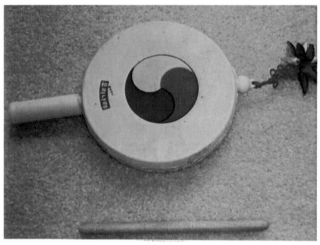

Sogo
(Small Drum)

---

1.   William H. Harris and Judith S. Levey, <u>The New Columbia Encyclopedia.</u> (New York: Columbia University Press, 1975), 1496-1497.

Chinese Influence In Korean Musical Instruments

One of the ways Koreans classify their instruments comes directly from China. The same eight categories used to classify Chinese instruments (bamboo, gourd, silk, leather, stone, metal, wood and clay) are used in Korea. This is considered the old way, while a second method groups instruments according to the genres in which they are used.[2]

Korean zithers are clearly descended from Chinese long zithers. Examples are the *komungo* (six strings) and the *kayagum* (twelve strings) zithers. Although these two instruments are claimed as indigenous instruments, it is difficult to imagine that they are not associated with their Chinese counterparts. Likewise the *kum* and *sul* are direct descendants of the Chinese *ch'in* and *se*. Another chordophone, the *hageum*, is a direct descendant of the Chinese *huqin* and perhaps the *erhu*.[3]

An aerophone with unmistakable relatives in both China and Japan is a mouth organ called the *saeng* which has seventeen bamboo tubes inserted into a wooden air chamber. Its Chinese relative is the *sheng* while the Japanese version is called the *sho*.[4] Another important aerophone in both classical and folk music is the double-reed oboe called the *p'iri*. It has a small bamboo tube with a large reed. It's sound is somewhat like the Japanese *hichiriki* and the western treble saxophone.[5]

An idiophone which has a clear counterpart in China is the o. This instrument consists of a crouching tiger on a box. It has 27 saw-like teeth on its back which are struck with a bamboo stick. The stick is also used to strike the neck of the tiger for cueing purposes. In China this instrument is called the *yu*.[6]

Another Korean idiophone with Chinese connection is the *p'yon'gyong*, a set of stone chimes suspended from a rack. In China, this instrument of antiquity is called the *pien-ch'ing*. A rack of 16 bells in China and Korea also show a common ancestry. In Korea the set is called *p'yonjong* while in China it is called *pien-chung*.[7]

---

2. Byong Won Lee, "Korea," New Grove's Dictionary of Music and Musicians. 20 vols., ed. Stanley Sadie (London: Macmillan, 1980), 196.

3. William P.Malm, Music Cultures of the Pacific, the Near East, and Asia. (Upper Saddle River, New Jersey: Prentice-Hall, Inc., 1996) 209.

4. Byong Won Lee, "Korea," New Grove's Dictionary of Music and Musicians. 199.

5. Malm, Music Cultures of the Pacific, the Near East, and Asia. 209.

6. Ibid.

7. J. A. Van Aalst, Chinese Music. New York: Paragon Book Reprint Corp., 1966) 54.

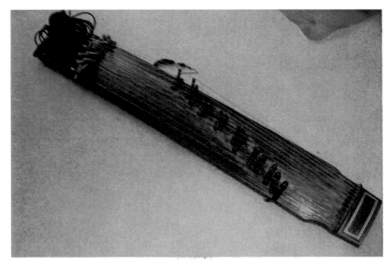

Kayagum
(Zither)

Piri
(Flute)

The main Korean membranophone is the *Changgo*. It is an elaborately decorated hour-glass shaped drum which is similar to the Japanese *o-tsuzumi* and *ko-tsuzumi* and the Chinese *chang ku*. There are numerous barrel-shaped drums which correspond to Chinese and Japanese models. The Korean versions are the *chwago,yonggo, puk, kyobanggo, cholgo, chin'go, nogo, nodo, sogo,* and *popko*.[8]

8.   Byong Won Lee, "Korea," New Grove's Dictionary of Music and Musicians. 199.

The Uniqueness of Korean Music

In spite of long periods of Chinese dominance and periods of intrusion from its Mongolian and Manchurian neighbors, Korea managed to maintain many of its ancient traditions as well as developing indigenous genres and styles. Chinese and Buddhist influence are undeniably a part of the Korean landscape and can be readily observed in architecture, art, and music, and particularly in musical instruments as has been previously demonstrated. And even though Korea and China both use pentatonic scales in their music, the disposition of the five tones is markedly different as is the music based on them. Likewise, the eight types of notation used in Korea, though heavily indebted to Chinese models, have been remodeled to accommodate the unique requirements of indigenous Korean music. In many ways, Korean music, like Korean food, can be said to be rather spicy and un-Oriental, characteristics, which along with the many foreign influences throughout its history, have served to create a unique and vibrant culture which distinguishes it from its neighbors.[9]

Kwengari
(Small gong)

9.   Malm, <u>Music Cultures of the Pacific, the Near East, and Asia,</u> 214.

Jing
(Gong)

Buk
(Medium Drum)

Bahasa Indonesian Musik

CHAPTER 10

Indonesia

Indonesia

Indonesia is a part of an extensive Malay archipelago made up of thousands of islands situated between the Indian and Pacific Oceans. Major Indonesian islands are Java, Bali, Sumatra, Borneo, Timor and Celebes. Indonesia was colonized by the Dutch in the 17th century and was also occupied by Japan from 1942 to 1945. In 1950 it became the **Republic of Indonesia.** It has the distinction of being the largest archipelagic state and host to the world's largest Muslim population.

The Gamelan

The Gamelan, a generic term for orchestra or ensemble, is central to the character of Indonesian music. Gamelans range in size from just a few instruments to over seventy-five pieces. The essence of gamelan music is captured in the following statement by Mantle Hood and Hardja Susilo.

"Javanese Gamelan is comparable to only two things: moonlight and flowing water. It is pure and mysterious like moonlight; it is always the same and always changing like flowing water. It forms for our ears no song, this music, it is a state of being, such as moonlight itself that lies poured out over the land. It flows murmuring, tinkling, and gurgling like water in a mountain stream. Yet it is never monotonous. Sometimes the sounds flow faster and louder just as water also sometimes speaks more loudly in the night only to sink back again quietly."[1]

Gamelan Instrument

Like the many islands that make up the Malayan archipelago, there are thousands of gamelans in the region.

1.   Mantle Hood and Hardja Susilo, <u>Music of the Venerable Dark Cloud: the Javenese Gamelan</u> <u>Khjai Mendung</u>. (Los Angeles: UCLA Institute of Ethnomusicology, 1967).

The Colotomic Structure

The gamelan is governed by a colotomic structure, colotomic meaning essentially punctuation or way of ordering events. This ordering might also be viewed as a kind of layering or polyphonic stratification that plays out through a given cycle of beats with the cycle being repeated numerous times as the music progresses. The number of beats may vary anywhere from four, eight, sixteen, or more.

The following functions are in force in the gamelan as the music unfolds.

1. **Cantus Firmus**

    There is a fixed, main melody, a melodic nucleus that manifests itself throughout. It might be played by an instrument such as the *rebab, yarul,* or the *suling,* or the *sarod* or *slentem.*

2. **Elaboration**

    A number of other instruments in the gamelan will have the task of elaborating on the above nuclear melody. These instruments may consist of various metallaphones such as the *bonang,* or the *gender.* Many layers of elaboration may be woven around the nuclear melody.

3. **Interpunctuating Gongs**

    These metallaphones function as the inner timekeepers as they hammer out the metrical divisions of the cycles in the colotomic structure. Such instruments may play beats 2,4,8, or some other designated pulse within the cycle. The *kenong ,kempul* or *ketuk* might be used for this purpose.

4. **Gong Ageng**

    This large gong is the main timekeeper whose job is to alert other members of the ensemble when the cycle begins and ends. In a sixteen-unit colotomic structure, *gong ageng* would strike on beat sixteen, the last beat, which would signal the return of beat one.

Scales And Tuning

There are two basic scales or tuning systems found mainly in Java and Bali. One is a pentatonic (five-tone) scale called *slendro,* and the other is a heptatonic (seven-tone) scale called *pelog.* Neither of these scales is governed by fixed pitches. In fact the pitches are highly variable from one gamelan to another, so much so that they cannot be rendered on the five lines and four spaces of the Western staff. Graph paper offers a better approximation of the actual pitches.[2]

This idea is based on Alexander Ellis' model of the Cents System. Ellis set the twelve semitones of the octave at 100 cents each, the octave therefore equaling 1200 cents. As shown on the graph, the pitches of a typical Indonesian pentatonic scale will fall somewhere in between the pitches of the Western scale. While closer than any other method outside of sophisticated electronic equipment, this method, like any other, will have its limitations.

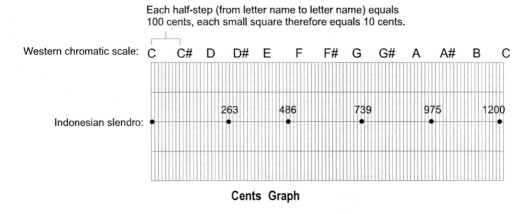

Cents Graph

Indonesian tunings are not standard with A at 440. Indonesians like a kind of shimmering effect in their music, and this is achieved by tuning one gamelan and even smaller instruments within a gamelan slightly different from another. Attempts to standardize pitch at A = 440 have never been successful.[3]

An Indonesian Aesthetic

To speak of an Indonesian aesthetic is problematic for reasons already alluded to in the discussion of the geography and the highly variable gamelan throughout Indonesian. **Bhinneka Tunggal Ika (*Unity in Diversity)*** is offered as the motto of Indonesia. It bespeaks the high variability found throughout the geography and cultures of the region. Given the fact that there are countless thousands of islands, this alone speaks to the wide range of possibilities to be found. In music and art, the range is from the most primitive on some of the more remote islands to rather sophisticated cultures on such islands as Java and Bali.[4]

Given this wide range of diversity, an aesthetic view of the Javanese and Balinese gamelan can nevertheless be obtained and is captured in the following statement by Collin McPhee.

---

2.   William Alves, <u>Music of the Peoples of the World</u>. 2nd. Ed. (Boston,Massachusetts: Schirmer Cengage Learning, 2009) 218.

3.   James Patrick O'Brien<u>, Non-Western Music and the Western Listener,</u> Dubuque, Iowa: Kendall/ Hunt Publishing Co., 1977) 79-80.

4.   <u>Ibid.</u>

A mystic, perfumed atmosphere surrounds the Javanese Gamelan, whose soft, shockless resonance has been refined to the ultimate degree of perfection. In strong contrast the Balinese gamelan stands out dramatically in its hard, metallic vitality and the almost feverish intensity with which the newer music is performed. 5

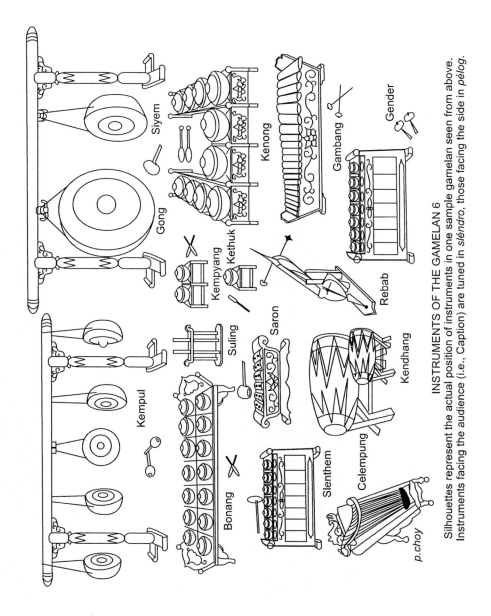

INSTRUMENTS OF THE GAMELAN 6

Silhouettes represent the actual position of instruments in one sample gamelan seen from above. Instruments facing the audience (i.e., Caption) are tuned in *sléndro*, those facing the side in *pélog*.

Labels: Siyem, Gong, Kenong, Kempyang, Kethuk, Gambang, Rebab, Gender, Kempul, Suling, Saron, Kendhang, Bonang, Slenthem, Celempung, p.choy

---

5. Collin McPhee, <u>Music in Bali</u> (New Haven: Yale University Press, 1966) 4.

6. Stephanie Morgan and Laurie J. Sears, eds. <u>Aesthetic Tradition and Cultural Transition in Java and Bali.</u> (Madison, Wisconsin: Center for Southeast Asian Studies-University of Wisconsin, 1984) 82.

Javanese Instruments

Chordophones

Rebab

The rebab is the most common chordophone. It is a two-string spiked fiddle and acts as a melodic leader.

Celempung

A large zither played with the fingernails.

Aerophones

Suling

The suling is a bamboo, end-blown duct flute.

Membranophones

Kendang

Kendang consists of two drums, a small one called *ketipung* and a large one called *kendang gending*.

Idiophones

Saron

One of many metallaphones found in the gamelan. They exist in three sizes an octave apart. The lowest is the *saron demung,* the next highest the *saron barung,* and the highest the *saron panerus* also called *peking.*

Gender

A xylophone-like metallaphone with tube resonators beneath its keys. The two sizes are the larger *gender barung,* and the *gender panerus* which is an octave higher in pitch. A felt-covered mallet produces a soft tone.

Slentem

This is the large, bass version of gender-type instruments, with xylophone-like keys and tube resonators. It is played with one large mallet rather than two.

Gambang

This is another xylophone-like instrument which is not a metallaphone. The wooden keys are played in parallel octaves. It has a box resonator and when played with two felt-wrapped mallets produces a light, delicate sound.

Bonang

One of a group of knobbed-pot gongs. In three-octave sets the lowest would be *bonang panembung,* the middle octave *bonang barung,* and the highest octave *bonang panerus.*

Kenong

A larger member of the knobbed-pot kettle gong family. Like the bonangs they are situated horizontally on strings.

Kempul

These are vertical suspended kettle gongs of a smaller size than the larger Gong Ageng.

Gong Ageng

The largest of the suspended, vertical gongs whose job is somewhat limited to indicating the end of the colotomic cycle. [7]

Balinese Instruments

Cantus firmus Metallaphones/Gongs

Penyacah

The highest-pitched of a group of metallaphones that play the nuclear melody.

---

7.   William Alves, Music of the Peoples of the World. 2nd Ed.. [Boston, Massachusetts: Schirmer Cengage Learning, 2009] 220-221.

Calung

> Middle-range metallaphones an octave lower than the *penyacah* that also participate in the cantus firmus.

Jegogan

> The lowest-pitched metallaphones of the cantus firmus group.

Elaborating Metallaphones

Gangsa

> A collective term for xylophone-like metallaphones that play elaborations on the nuclear melody and which include the following:
>
> *Kantilan* - four xylophone-like instruments.
>
> *Pemade* - metallaphone similar to the kantilan sounding an octave lower.
>
> *Ugal* - leader of the gangsa section playing both the cantus firmus and elaborations.
>
> Gongs
> *Large gong* - suspended.
> *Kempur* - medium suspended gong.
> *Kentong* - high-pitched suspended gong.
> Kempli - a knobbed-pot gong that maintains the pulse.

A Unique Metallaphone

Reyong

> *A* horizontally-mounted set of twelve gongs played by four people.

Cymbals

Ceng-Ceng

> *A* set of cymbals situated with their bottoms attached to the back of a replica of a turtle. They act as reinforcers of the drum patterns and may be played by one or two people. [8]

---

8.   Ibid.. 236.

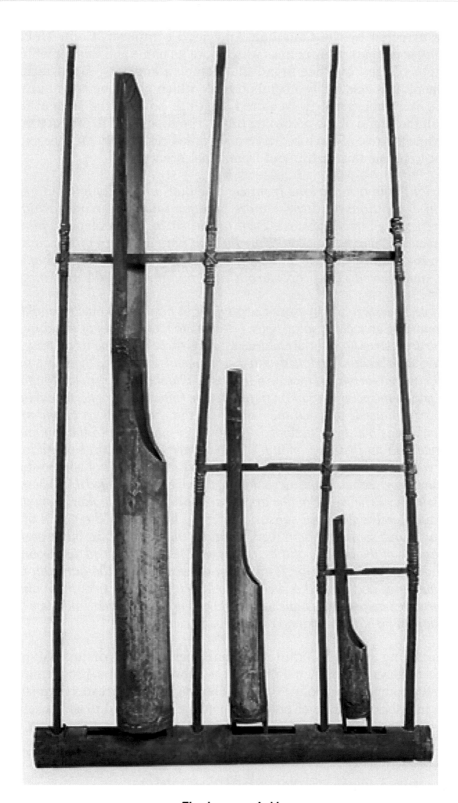

The Javanese Anklung

A very unique instrument which was at one time on the verge of extinction was resurrected by the Canadian-American composer, Colin McPhee. The *angklung* was a part of ensembles which bore its name and was sometimes found in remote villages. McPhee found that gamelan angklung rarely included this instrument. It is essentially a bamboo rattle which plays one pitch in two to four octaves, each tube cut at the required length to produce the pitch at the octave (one half the length of the preceding tube). The tube is cut to produce the desired pitch while the rest of the tube serves as a tuned resonator[9]. McPhee explains his attempt to rescue this instrument from obsolescence.

> *Bright young musicians from central Bali who accompanied me on my expeditions to these remote villages found their old-fashioned orchestras utterly absurd. They would sit in polite silence while the musicians played, but could hardly wait until we drove off to comment on the "plain" . . . style of the music, the "stiff" .. . way of playing, and to gaily parody the preposterous accompaniment of the angkhmgs.*

> *Nevertheless, when in 1938 I organized in Sayan a gamelan angklung composed entirely of small boys, I decided to include a set of angklungs in the orchestra. At first the children ignored these instruments entirely, but they soon became intrigued with their unusual sound, and there was much discussion—in which I took no part—as to who should play them. I engaged a young musician from Karangasem [the remote area where angklungs were still used] to teach the club and train the four boys to whom the angklungs had been assigned. These latter caught on to the unfamiliar style with sur prising rapidity. Within a few months this club of children— a complete novelty in Bali—had acquired a repertory of compositions, some short, some of considerable length, which they played with complete assurance. Their first public appearance at a temple odalan [festival] in Sayan created a local sensation, partly because of the youth of the musicians, some of whom were no more than five or six, but especially because of the novelty of the angklungs. The word spread, and soon the club was in demand for festivals in other villages; the gamelan with angklungs had proved a success. Today [1966], I am told, these almost forgotten instruments have become familiar to every-one, and have been adopted by other angklung orchestras in central Bali.[10]*

Angklung playing is quite like handbell playing or jug playing. Each instrument plays its designated pitch at the appropriate time, producing what can be called a composite melody. This distribution of notes creates both simple and also an interlocking fabric of pitches which is also referred to as hocket style.[11]

---

9. Bruno Nettl, et.al., <u>Excursions in World Music</u> (Upper Saddle river, New Jersey: Pearson-Prentice Hall, 2004) 161.

10. Colin McPhee, <u>Music in Bali</u> (New York: Da Capo, 1976) 243.

11. Arved M.Larsen, <u>Crossroads in Music</u> (Belmont, California: Thomson-Schirmer, 2003)114.

Dramatic Genres

Wayang Kulit

A *wayang* is a dramatic presentation. *Wayang kuit* is a specific type of dramatic presentation, namely, the shadow puppet play. This title is descriptive due to the fact that the audience sees only the shadows of the puppets projected onto a screen, and not the actual puppets themselves. The puppets are elaborately carved from leather in exquisite detail which renders the projected shadows quite convincing. The plays are often based on the Mahabharata and Ramayana epics of ancient Hindu tradition. [12]

The central figure in the puppet play is the *dalang* or puppeteer who is virtually a one-man show. He is a well-trained, highly skilled individual who not only manipulates the puppets which can number in the hundreds, but is also the narrator and provides the various voice parts as the dialogue and dramatic action progresses. Political commentary, gossip and satyre may also issue forth from the *dalang* [13]   Good and evil are portrayed in conflict with each other with the good characters visibly represented on the left of the audience and the evil to the audience's right. A Wagnerian-like leitmotif relationship often exists between the characters and instruments in the gamelan. It is not uncommon for puppet plays to last through the night concluding with a triumph over evil around daybreak. [14]

Kecak

Kecak is another dramatic form of entertainment. Although it has roots in *sanghyang,* a religious trance dance, and the *Ramayana* epic, the ancient significance of these has now faded in favor of a form which is essentially entertainment for tourists. Walter Spiess, a German painter and perhaps Colin McPhee, a Canadian-American composer were instrumental in the evolution of this genre.

Kecak, or monkey chant, is in fact performed by a group of men who imitate the sounds of a band of chattering monkeys after the manner of the layering and polyphonic stratification of the instruments of the gamelan. One can hear an unmistakable imitation of the gamelan in this performance. Even though it is no longer used for exorcizing demons, there is still a quasi-religious character apparent in the actions of a sexton who recites a prayer and offers incense, flowers, and holy water in preparation for the event. The *Ramayana*

---

12. Claire Holt. Art in Indonesia (New York: Cornell University Press. 1967). 267-273.   ~~

13. James O'Brien. Non-Western Music and the Western Listener (Dubuque. Iowa: Kendall/Hunt Publishing Company, 1977) 93.

14. Ibid.

epic is still referenced, the age-old struggle between good and evil is reinacted, and the triumph of good over evil is retained with the return of peace to the earth. [15]

CODA

The rich diversity of musical styles in Indonesia is understandable given the many influences that have impacted the region throughout the centuries. Chinese contact with Indonesia can be documented as early as the Third century B.C. Next came Indian and Braham Hinduism in the first and second centuries A.D. The fifth century saw the appearance of Buddhism which eventually merged with indigenous cult traditions and Brahmanism. Islam appeared in the thirteenth century and by the fifteenth century was a dominant force. The sixteenth century onward saw an increase in Western influences, English, Dutch, Portuguese, and others. Arab, Mongol, and Chinese contact resulted from trade and military conflict. The impact of all of these cultures, along with many others along the Southeast Asian chain, has produced a mosaic of cultural and musical parameters which are as rich and varied as the vast expanse of the thousands of islands of which the Indonesian archipelago is comprised. [16]

15, JVC Video Anthology of World Music and Dance [Southeast Asia V - Tape 10, Indonesia 2] (Montpelier, Vermont: New England Networks, 1991).

16 William P. Malm, Music Cultures of the Pacific, the Near East, and Asia (Upper Saddle River, New Jersey: Prentice Hall, Inc., 1996) 43.

Latin America

(Hispanic Music)

Español de Música

Español de Música

Español de Música

CHAPTER 11

Latin America

Latin America

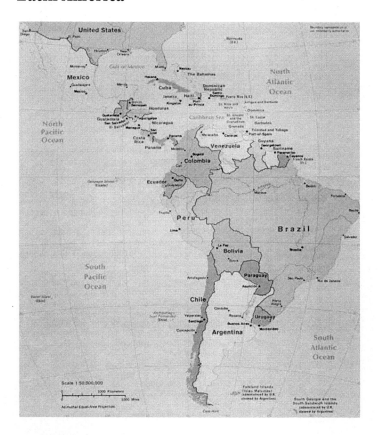

Geography And History

     The word mestizo is apropos to a description and discussion of Latin America, for it is indeed a complex mixture of cultures and traditions. The Columbian myth regarding the discovery of America is just that, and is part of a history that needs to be rewritten. If Columbus discovered anything, it was that the people who were here when he arrived were part of ancient civilizations who came to the region some thirty-five to forty thousand years ago, even by conservative estimates. There is considerable evidence in support of a pre-Columbian presence throughout what is now called the Americas, the inhabitants having come across the Bering Straights when it was a frozen "land bridge" in the late Pleistocene age. Waves of migrations continued as they filtered down from the North Pole, perhaps through Siberia and down toward Mongolia, eventually moving over to Alaska, and then into Canada, and eventually into what is now North, Central, and South America. The Indian label assigned to these peoples by Columbus is a misnomer, probably due to the fact that Columbus was not altogether sure where he was, and having heard something about the Indies in this part of the world, decided to call those he encountered Indians.

Pre-Columbian culture in Latin America was derived from three ancient civilizations, namely, the Aztecs, the Incans, and the Mayans. These civilizations were highly developed in mathematics, astronomy, architecture, and music, to name a few. Remnants of these civilizations exist side by side with influences from Spain and Portugal and from Africa. These mestizo cultures have produced a modern-day cultural fabric that bespeaks the cultural fusion or syncretism that has resulted from the impact of these cultures upon each other.

While there are many ethnic groups throughout South America and including Mexico, Central America, and the Caribbean, Spanish and Roman Catholicism are linguistic and religious unifying elements. There are, however, indigenous languages still being spoken, and both indigenous and African influences manifest themselves in language, religious, and other cultural aspects. Religious syncretism is further evidenced in the combining of African deities with Catholic saints, and musical syncretism is clearly evident in the fusion of indigenous, European and African instruments.[1]

Musical Syncretism

Indigenous And European

Given the issues of syncretism discussed above, any discussion of musical instruments must necessarily reference the influence of indigenous, European, and African elements. Prehistoric, indigenous instruments would have included conch shells, ocarinas, whistles, slit drums, flutes, and rattles made out of such things as cocoons, metal, and deer hooves. A *guiro* or rasp made out of a human bone or some other material would have existed. Other indigenous instruments can be seen in the Andean highlands particularly in Southern Peru and Bolivia amongst the Quechua and the Aymara. These would include the following:

---

1.   William Alves, <u>Music of the Peoples of the World</u> (Belmont, California: Thomson-Schirmer, 2006) 282.

kenas	vertical kane flutes
siku	panpipes
pinkillus and *tarkas*	recorder-like flutes
pitus	side-blown flutes
wankara or *bombos*	large double-headed drums
cajas	large indigenous snaredrum

In indigenous practice, vocal music is rare, and stringed instruments were not used prior to the coming of the conquistodores who brought with them the harp, the violin, and the guitar which appears in many sizes from miniature to the large bass version called the guitarron. A popular type adopted by the Aymara is the *charango* sometimes made out of the body of an armadillo.[2]

African Retentions And Influence

In addition to these indigenous instruments and European adaptations, considerable African influence can be readily observed in parts of Latin America.

A number of characteristics of African Music as outlined in Chapter 3 under Sub-Saharan Africa have been retained in the music of the African Diaspora, if not the original forms, then certainly some adaptations of these characteristics are present. Musical retentions are but one instance of Africanisms transported to this hemisphere. The musical retentions as well as other traits are a natural result of the cultural transplant effected through the slave trade.

It is generally thought by scholars and those outside the academic community that the slaves who came to this country came from the coast of West Africa and its hinterland. If this were the case, the problem of tracking down the spread of Africanisms to the'Western hemisphere would be far less formidable. However, Professor Ivan Van Sertima maintains that Blacks also came from areas other than the coast of West Africa. He states,

> *The Blacks of this hemisphere did not come, as is still popularly believed, only from West Africa. The Guinea coast was just the transit center for slaves. Some African slaves of the American south were from the Lower Congo, whose people were largely in the Bantu culture complex. There is evidence, too, that during the first quarter of the nineteenth century slaves were frequently imported from Mozambique and other parts of the eastern coast. 'Mombasos' (Kenyans) are known to have*

---

2.   Bruno Nettl, et.al., Excursions in World Music (Upper Saddle River, New Jersey: Pearson-Prentice Hall, 2008) 284-285.

been mentioned by the Negro slaves in Cuba and many cargoes of
slaves were smuggled from Havana into the Southern States after the
import trade was declared illegal.[3]

If this is true, African traits in this hemisphere must first be identified as
Africanisms, but then it must be determined from what part of that vast
composite of great stylistic diversity such elements may have derived.

Other recent scholarship has provided evidence for an African presence in
this hemisphere in pre-Columbian times. It is known that Africans from Mali
came to this hemisphere in 1310.[4] Skeletal remains of African magicians, the
existence of black gods in the Amerindian pantheon (e.g. Ixtliton, "the one with
the black face" and also Ekchuah, "the black god of the Mexicans and Mayas,")
are all indisputable evidence of that presence. Negro heads found in Mexico predate
the conquistador arrival. This archeological evidence is most valuable for
establishing a pre-Columbian African presence.[5] The botanical evidence for an
African-New World exchange is likewise convincing. African strains of cotton
came to this hemisphere while maize was transported to Africa, an exchange
which could only have taken place as a result of trans-Atlantic voyages. Objections
have been raised to the effect that such trans-Atlantic voyages were not possible
before the Columbian voyages. Recent evidence has again demonstrated that
historical facts are not in sympathy with such objections.[6] Small boats from
Africa have crossed the Atlantic over one hundred times, an African dug-out being
one of those boats.[7]

It is clear, then, that there is overwhelming archeological, botanical, and
nautical evidence in support of an African presence in the New World in pre-
Columbian times. It is also clear that the matter of African retentions in the music
of the African Diaspora in the New World has far deeper roots and significance
than those who support the "Columbian myth" (i.e. that Columbus discovered
America) would care to admit.

Another problem which makes it extremely difficult to deal with the history
of Black folk prior to their arrival on this continent as slaves, and even for some
time afterwards, is the fact that we are dealing with an oral culture about which
very little has been written. A rediscovery of that oral tradition is necessary if the

---

3. Ivan Van Sertima, "African Folk Archetypes In The New World," an unpublished paper (Evanston: Northwestern University, n.d.), 21-22.

4. Jan carew,"The Origins of Racisms in America," an unpublished manuscript (Evanston Northwestern University, n.d.),3.

5. <u>Ibid</u>., 1.

6. <u>Ibid</u>., 4.

7. Ibid., 5.

distortions and omissions of Western scholarship relative to Africa and the African Diaspora are to be corrected. Jan Carew is thoroughly dedicated to that task. He very eloquently states his concern as follows:

> There is a living monument to Africa in the Black American himself. Civilizations can sometimes survive in the human person, in living men, not merely in stone and wood, brass and steel. That living civilization, that vital essence and nucleus of the international black experience, may be found, for example in the rich oral tradition of the black people - in the language, in the myths, in the value systems and metaphysics of the folklore.[8]

Music becomes extremely important in this regard, for as Carew points out:

> The richest depository of that oral tradition, the most enduring witness of buried black life, submerged black structures, are in speech, music and folklore.[9]

The question of these African roots in the music of the New World African Diaspora is one which has been the subject of heated and extended debate. There have been those on the one hand who maintained that Africans brought nothing with them to this hemisphere except their strong bodies and empty minds, hungry for the civilization of their oppressors, and that anything they accomplished or produced after that was directly attributable to their European derived hosts. On the other hand, there were those (Sir Harry Johnson and Melville Herskovits) who took the opposite position, namely, that the slaves brought their own unique style of music with them to this hemisphere. They also brought with them a way of thinking about music which on the one hand they maintained and developed, while on the other they incorporated elements from their foreign surroundings into their own music.[10] Various authors continued to maintain different positions, some taking extreme positions on either side while others tended more toward a middle ground. The most adamant author against any origiinality in Negro music was George Pullen Jackson, who made every effort to discredit any notion of originality in words or music in Negro folk music.[11] The controversy as it emanated from Walloschek, Henry Krehbiel, Newman Ivy White, George Pullen Jackson, Hornbostel and other writers in the field seemed to settle around two alternatives:

(1) Either the Negro slaves and their descendants copied the songs that were all around them or

---

8. Jan Carew, "African American Studies - A Position Paper," unpublished manuscript (Evanston: Northwestern University, 1972), 2-3,

9. Ibid.

10. Richard Alan Waterman, "On Flogging a Dead Horse: Lessons Learned from the Africanisms Controversy," Journal of Ethnomusicology, VII/2 (May, 1963), 83.

11. Ibid., 84f.

(2) perhaps by virtue of a truly remarkable racial musical talent they invented them out of nothing in order to express the emotions proper to slaves and depressed peoples. The first alternative was embraced by Walloschek, White, and Jackson while the latter was supported by Krehbiel and Hornbostel.

The problem was brought into clearer focus by Waterman who insisted on the following factors:

(1) The development of an anthropological theory concerning acculturation, (2) an increasing knowledge of characteristics of West African music, (3) a realization that the Negro of the United States formed a part of the so called Afro-American culture which included Negro subcultures in South America and the Caribbean, as well as North America, (4) the gradual abandonment of such concepts as racial musical talent, and (5) an awareness that music is an aspect of culture, and functions as one. [12]

Once these factors were recognized, the question changed from, "Did the American Negro invent his folk music or did he copy it?" to, "How did the musical heritage of the West African change over generations of contact with alien musical forms?"[13] The importance of Waterman's contribution was that it demonstrated that pre-existing notions about alien cultures often prevented the kind of reinterpretation necessary to the proper understanding of the blending of different culture patterns.[14] With this understanding, a new and more productive approach became possible.

African Influences in Latin America and the Caribbean

From a broader perspective African retentions are far more pronounced and identifiable in Latin America and the Caribbean than in North America. Things African were tolerated a great deal more south of Mexico because of strong Amerindian influence and the Roman Catholic Church, this due mainly to the fact that American Indians were not at all the savage, hostile beasts they have been portrayed to be, but rather gracious hosts until otherwise provoked by European invaders. Also, the Roman Catholic Church was more willing to allow for religious syncretism than were their North American Protestant counterparts. North of Mexico, Africanisms among the slaves were discouraged, forbidden, outlawed, and severely punished by brutal and inhumane taskmasters. Nevertheless, Africanisms did survive, though to a lesser degree, even under such unfavorable conditions.

---

12. Ibid., 84f.

13. Ibid.

14. Ibid.

African characteristics are more apparent in the cult music of Black folk in Latin America and the Caribbean and less important in the worksongs, social dance songs, narrative songs and love songs. Bruno Nettl outlines the cults of African origins which can be found throughout the Caribbean.

> *In Haiti, similar kinds of cults exist; among them are <u>Vodoun</u> (origin of the word 'voodoo'), which is built around the religious practices of Nigerian and Dahomean tribes; <u>Ibo</u>, named after a Nigerian tribe; <u>Salongo</u>; Juba, essentially a social dance which once had religious significance, and which was known in the other islands and even in New Orleans; and Petro (which may be named after one of several historical personages named Pedro). Some of these ceremonies are parts of an elaborate ritual cycle known as the Congo-Guinea cycle; all include singing and dancing.* [15]

Offshoots of these cults are very much alive throughout the Caribbean and in rural and urban centers in the United States.

Another source for the study of Africanisms in this hemisphere is the drums, which are similar to those in Africa, and drumming practices associated with these instruments. Many of the drums, the beaters used with them, and various other rhythmic instruments found in this hemisphere are of unmistakable African origin. Nettl describes the drums and their beaters.

> *. . . The drums found in Cuba, Haiti, Trinidad, Surriname, Venezuela and Brazil are made in numerous designs of West African provenience. Square drums resembling those of the Ashanti of the Gold Coast and the Baya of French Equatorial Africa have been reported in Jamaica. Square drums appear also to have been known in New Orleans. The peg-type drum familiar in West Africa and the Congo, are found in Haiti, Trinidad, other West Indian islands, and South America. The Yoruba two-headed <u>bata</u> drums are important instruments in the Lucumi cult of Cuba. The paired drums held over the knee—a familiar sight in Cuba and other Latin American countries—appear to be related to similar but larger drums found in the Ivory coast. Some of the Arada drums (of Dahomean provenience) still to be seen in museums in Cuba and Haiti are ornately carved and decorated in the African manner. Other African instruments such as the stamping tube (made of a length of hollow bamboo), the friction drum, the inverted flared bell, and the slit-log-signal-drum are also to be found in the Americas. The African friction drum is used by the Carabali society in Cuba. The stamping tubes are known and used in Haiti under the name <u>ganbos</u> and in*

---

15. Bruno Nettl, <u>Folk and Traditional Music of the Western Continents </u>(New Jersey: Prentice-Hall, 1965), 173.

*Venezuala under the name of quitiplas. The slit-log signal drum
survived in Haiti in somewhat revised form until recent years, and a
miniature version is still used by the Cuban Lucumi (Yoruba) cult.*

*. . . Not only have the West African drum forms persisted, but even the
sticks which are used to beat them remain, in many cases, true to the
prototypes. Some of them are straight, some hooked at the beating
end, and some are mallet-shaped. Throughout a large part of Negro
America are to be found gourd and calabash rattles, metal rattles and
wicker or basket-shaped rattles—all of African origin. [16]*

The quote, though lengthy, provides many specific details as to the
construction of these drums and beaters, details which unmistakably identify them
as African in origin.

Even in the continental United States, African-type drums may be found.
Harold Courlander describes some of these instruments.

A survey conducted in the Sea Islands of Georgia only a relatively few
years ago produced evidence that persons then alive recalled the use of
drums for dances and death rites. In Alabama in 1950 I found the
remains of an old peg-type drum being used as a storage container for
chicken feed. It is probable that the persistent use of the shallow
tambourine or finger drum by certain Negro groups stems as much
from African tradition as from European. In secular folk music, the
wash-tub bass is played precisely in the manner of the African earth
bow: the string is plucked and beaten by one player, while a second
player beats on the inverted tub as though it were a drum. [17]

Not only do the instruments themselves survive but also the attitudes toward
them and the manner of playing them. Courlander describes these performance
practices.

Where the African drum survives, so do playing techniques and
attitudes. Instruments with goatskin heads are played with the hands,
while those with cowhide heads are beaten with sticks. Where drums
are played in batteries, each drum has its well-defined part, and usually
there is a gourd rattle to mark the time. Sometimes a metal percussion
device supplements the drums. The player of the larger drums sometimes
beats his stick on the wooden side for additional effects. The practice of
the player sitting astride the drum and muting the head with a heel is

16, Ibid., 175ff.

17. Harold Courlander, <u>African and Afro-American Drums</u>. Ethnic Folkways Library (New York:
Folkways Records and Service Corp., 1962) 1.

well known in the West Indies. In Haiti the Juba drum is played in this manner, with a second player beating two sticks against the wood behind the drummer. In the Virgin Islands the Bamboula drums are played in this style. All of these characteristics are African.[18]

It should be kept in mind that African drums, rhythms, and performance practices have not survived in the New World as separate entities, but, as in Africa, tend to be associated with many other aspects of the musical experience, such as the dance, certain ritual observances, and so on. Very strong African characteristics can also be seen through an organological survey of instruments other than drums. In Haiti, the following can be observed:

> Among the idiophones, the <u>ogan</u>, a kind of iron bell struck with an external clapper, is prominent, as are gourd rattles. The <u>mosquito drum</u> (a type of drum not mentioned earlier] a type of musical bow, of which one end is attached to the ground while the other extends a string attached to a piece of skin covering a hole in the ground, is used as an accompaniment to singing. In this instrument, the hole in the ground functions as a resonance chamber, much as the calabash or the player's mouth aides resonance to the sound of musical bows in Southern and Central Africa.[19]

Other instruments which are clearly of African origin can be found in the Caribbean. The instruments are described as follows:

> Stamping tubes, hollow tubes struck on the ground or on a board, provide another kind of rhythmic accompaniment. A rather large and deep-sounding version of the African <u>sansa</u> or <u>mbira</u> (called marimba in Haiti) is also found in the Caribbean. Horns and trumpets made of bamboo, each capable of playing only one pitch, are used, as are cow's horns, conch-shell trumpets, and horns improvised from various objects such as phonograph loudspeaker horns. The <u>claves</u>, short sticks made of hardwood and struck together with the use of one hand, are important in the Caribbean. The xylophone, common in Africa, is not as widespread in the Afro-American cultures but does seem to have become one of the important instruments of Central America. In Guatemala, the marimba (xylophone with gourd resonators) has become a national instrument.[20]

Another type of instrument which is generally referred to as a 'drum' but is more properly classified as a percussion idiophone is the steel drum of Trinidad. Nettl describes this instrument as follows:

---

18. <u>Ibid.</u>, 2.

19. Nettl, <u>Folk and Traditional Music of the Western Continents</u>, 176-178

20. <u>Ibid.</u>, 178,

The steel drum, an instrument invented in Trinidad during or after World War II, is a fascinating example of the results of the acculturation of African practices in modern Western civilization. Steel oil containers, abandoned and available, their tops hammered into shapes producing the desired scales, were combined into groups of three or four different sizes and accompanied rhythmically by idiophones, rattles, calvess, or bells. The bottom sections of the containers were cut off later, and the steel drums were placed on special stands. Each 'drum' is capable of playing simple melodic material. The result is music of a strongly rhythmic character, with polyphony of an ostinato nature, and with each 'drum' (or 'pan' as they are called by the players) having a particular musical function, as in a jazz band."[21]

These drums are a perfect example of the adaptations which arose when African-derived people were deprived of their native instruments and musical practices. The steel drum recalled for them both the African drum and xylophone in that it functions as both a melodic and rhythmic instrument.

The following account underscores the ingenuity of these homemade instruments.

> *At first, they used cookie tins and garbage can lids, to the annoyance of other local residents, who complained so much about the noise that for a time there was a ban on such ensembles. But the so-called steel band enthusiasts were not so easily discouraged. They turned their attention from tins and trash cans to old oil drums, which form the basis of most steel bands today.*
>
> *Turning the oil drums into pitched or semi-pitched percussion instruments is done in several stages. The bottom of the drum, with no tap hole in it, is the part that matters. The potential drumhead is first hammered into a concave shape, which improves its tone. Further indentations may then be hammered into the surface, each of which, if the job is skillfully done, can sound a note of different pitch. The length or height of the supporting drum cylinder, it should be added, determines the overall pitch of the instrument. Finally, the drum needs to be tempered by heating and cooling rapidly with cold water.*
>
> *The homemade ingenuity of steel or pan bands extends to the drum sticks. These have often been made by stretching a section of the inner tube of an old bicycle tire over a wooden stick.* [22]

---

21. Ibid., 178-180.

22. Alan Blackwood, <u>Music of the World,</u> (Englewood Cliffs, New Jersey: Prentice-Hall Incorporated, 1991) 105.

Flamenco Influence In The Americas

Flamenco is a style of music and dance that came out of Andalusia in the southern part of Spain. It is thought to have come from North Africa as Arab-speaking people entered Spain, but may also have arrived in Spain with the Gypsies from the north or the east. Since the word flamenco can mean Flemish, it is reasonable to assume that the Gypsies entered Spain from the Low Countries to the north. Flamenco includes styles of singing, dancing and guitar playing. Finger snapping and foot stamping with erect posture are characteristic of the dance style, while strumming and passage work are characteristic of the guitar style. The singing style is also distinctive and is characterized as deep song *(jondo* or *cante hondo).*

The influence of *flamenco* can be found in some forms of Mexican dance. It can also be found in a dance done by the **gouchos,** the cowboys of Argentina called the **malambo**[23]

Mariachi

Mariachi is a kind of music played originally by three to twelve players of string instruments which included violins, guitars, mandolins, and double basses. An occasional flute was used and brass instruments were added later. Perhaps the name *mariachi* comes from the French word *mariage* as the ensembles were often used at weddings.[24]

It is thought that *mariachi* string bands originated in Jalisco, a state in west central Mexico. These ensembles can be heard on the streets and in cafes throughout the country. [25] The most common chorophones used were violins, a small guitar with five strings called the *vihuela,* a large bass guitar called the *guitarron* and an occasional harp. The brass component when used consisted of trumpets and trombones. [26]

23. Don Rondel, "Flamenco." <u>Harvard Dictionary of Music,</u> (Cambridge, Mass.: Harvard University Press, 1986), 310.

24. Bruno Nettl et.al., <u>Excursions in World Music,</u> 5th. Ed., (Upper Saddle River, New Jersey: Pearson/Prentice-Hall, 2008), 282-283.

25. Bruno Nettl, <u>Folk and Traditional Music of the Western Continents,</u> (Englewood Cliffs, New Jersey: Prentice-Hall Incorporated, 1965), 192.

26. Ibid.

Latin Rhythms

Rhythm	Country
Bambuco	Columbia
Bolero	Cuba
Bossa Nova	Brazil
Cha-Cha-Cha	Cuba
Cueca	Chile
Cumbia	Colombia
Danza	Cuba
Guaracha	Cuba
Jarabe	Mexico
Joropo	Venezuela
Malambo	Argentina
Mambo	Cuba
Merengue	Dominican Republic
Paso Doble	Spain
Porro	Colombia
Ranchera	Mexico
Rhumba	Afro-Cuban
Samba	Brazil
Tango	Argentina

Latin American Musical Instruments

Idiophones

Shaken Idiophones

    Maracas (gourd)

    Maracas (wooden)

Struck Together Idiophones

    Claves

Struck *Idiophone*

    Steel Drum

    Marimba

Scraped Idiophones

    Reso-Reso (Bamboo Scraper from Mexico)

    Horn Scraper (Mexico)

    Quijada (Jawbone)

Membranophones

Drums

    Bongos

    Conga Drum

    Cuica (friction drum)

    Timbales

    Bomba

Aerophones

Straight-Plain Aerophones

    Siku (Panpipes)

    Kena (notched horizontal flute)

Chordophones

Lutes

> *Charango* (Made from the shell of an armadillo)
>
> *Requinto*   (Small Guitar)
>
> *Jarana*   (Medium-sized Guitar)
>
> *Guitarron* (Bass Guitar)
>
> *Bandolin*   (From the Spanish Mandolin)

Harp

> *Arpa* (Plays in one diatonic key)

Bandolin

Kenas

Kenas

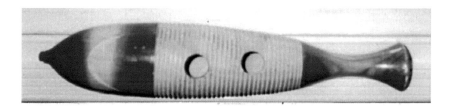

Guiro

Steel drum

Maracas

Maracas

Claves

Tubular Wood Block

Congas

Bongos

CHAPTER 12

Native America

In Chapter 11 we discussed Pre-Columbian cultures in what is now Latin America. This chapter will focus on the Native American groups that populated the region north of Mexico. It is estimated that there are as few as two hundred and as many as four hundred tribes remaining in North America. As they tend to remain fairy subdued, it is difficult to pinpoint either their locations or their activities. The following map by Harold Driver and others attempts to show the area distribution of musical style traits north of Mexico. While such a distributional

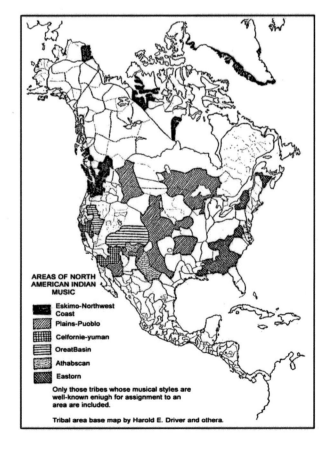

AREAS OF NORTH AMERICAN INDIAN MUSIC

- Eskimo-Northwest Coast
- Plains-Puoblo
- Celfornie-yuman
- OreatBasin
- Athabscan
- Eastorn

Only those tribes whose musical styles are well-known eniugh for assignment to an area are included.

Tribal area base map by Harold E. Driver and othera.

attempt is problematic due to the many social, cultural, and linguistic parameters involved, it nevertheless offers a general picture of a large area of cultures as distributed throughout North America.[1]

General Considerations

The six groups as indicated above must not be viewed as if etched in stone. There are other groups which do not coincide geographically or stylistically with these areas, and there are the usual issues with centers and borders and the inevitable overlapping and syncretism that ensues. Further complications arise from the fact that North American tribes have more often than not remained separate from their white and black counterparts with the advantage on the other hand of having preserved to much greater extent their aboriginal customs and musical styles. Given these and other difficulties, we cautiously proceed with a brief general description of cultures and traits north of Mexico.

Sound Sources

Unlike the plethora of instruments found south of Mexico, there are relatively few musical instruments north of Mexico. In contrast to the numerous instruments shown in Latin America in Chapter 11, the indigenous instruments north of Mexico can be counted on one hand. These instruments will be shown later

Connections To Nature

Another common trait north of Mexico can be found in the close relationship to and reverence for nature and all that dwells therein. This relationship is clearly evident in the names of persons and dance songs. Some of the most common are the Rabbit Dance, Turtle Dance, Snake Dance, and the Harvest Dance. Examples of social dances would be the Round Dance, the Sun Dance, and the Ghost Dance.

To Scale Or Not To Scale

Any discussion of scales, key, or any other theoretical issues must be approached with extreme caution. Points of entry between Native American music and European-derived musics are few and elusive and risky at best. The music has its own structure and purpose and probably should be compared as little possible with other musics. There is the obvious issue of indeterminate pitch and lack of pitch discrimination which is far removed from any convenient reference to the standard pitches of the Western piano. No one has spoken to the perils of applying such a standard any better than Frances Densmore of long ago.

---

1. Bruno Nettl, "North American Indian Musical Styles," The American Folklore Society, 45 (1954), 2.

The pitch of the piano is taken for convenience as the standard of pitch in Indian singing. Measured by that standard it is found that he sings a semitone with uncertain intonation and that a succession of whole - tones varies greatly in their intonation. The minor third is sung less clearly than the major third and, as already stated, his intonation is best on the fifth and the octave. In singing a long melody he seems to keep the boundary of the octave in his mind and, though the intervening intervals may vary, it will be found that two tones an octave apart are in good intonation. If he possessed a musical system with small intervals, it would be apparent in the phonograph records of hundreds of his songs. Instead, we find a reasonably correct use of the simplest upper partials or overtones of a fundamental, and uncertainty in singing semitones.[2]

In the same vein, any discussion of harmony in Native American music is moot, for any attempts to render this "non-harmonic" music on the piano are less than satisfactory. Attempts to harmonize the music clearly compromises the essence and charm of the music, hence the caveat against inappropriate comparisons.[3]

Language, Words, And Vocables

Native American languages are numerous and complex. Three major geographical divisions are indicated, namely, North American, Mexico and Central American, and South American and the West Indies. Estimates are that from the earliest European contacts, up to forty million people spoke up to 1,800 to 2,000 different languages. Recent estimates suggest 700 surviving languages spoken by

Eskimo-Aleut	Algonquian-Wakashan	Nadene
	Arapaho	Athabascan
	Blackfoot	(Navaaho and Apache)
	Cheyenne	Haida
	Cree	Tlingit
	Delaware	
	Ojibwa (Chippewa)	
	Sac	
	Fox	
	Flathead	
	Nootka	
	Kwakiutl	

---

2.   Frances Densmore. "Scale in Indian Music." <u>The American Indians and Their Music</u>.
     (New York: The Womans Press. 1926). 137-138.

3.   Ibid.

approximately twelve million people in Central and South America, and as few as 200 languages spoken by approximately 250,000 Native Americans in North America. 4 The North American groups are shown below with a few of their constituent tribes.

Penutian	Aztec-Tanoan	Hokan-Siouan
Maidu	Muskogean	Comanche
Wintun	Choctaw	Hopi
Yokuts	Chickasaw	Paiute
Chinook	Creek	Shoshone
	Seminole	Ute
		Zuni[5]

Caddoan
Caddo
Wichita
Pawnee
Arikara

Yuman
Cocopa
Mohave
Yuma

Iroquoian
Seneca
Cayuga
Mohawk
Oneida
Wyandot
Tuscarora

Siouan
Catawba
Winnebago
Osage
Dakota
Crow

The origins and interrelationships of these languages are still quite obscure in spite of numerous attempts in recent studies to demonstrate relationships between Native American and Asian and European languages. No doubt many languages from Mexico southward contained remnants from ancient civilizations that once inhabited the region, such as the Aztecs, Incans, and Mayans. However, attempts to decipher this progression have likewise encountered great difficulties.

---

4.   William H. Harris and Judith S. Levey, eds., The New Columbia Encyclopedia (NewYork: Columbia University Press, 1975) 85.

5.   Ibid.

Only after the coming of the Spaniards and missionaries were attempts made to subject these languages to an alphabetic system or written form since they previously existed and were preserved only through oral tradition.[6] The number, complexity, and possible origins of these languages all offer seemingly insurmountable obstacles. Perhaps new technologies and research techniques will allow for significant future breakthroughs.

We can only surmise that out of this complexity of languages arises the characteristic use of vocables or in some instances a combination of syllables and words. The vocabularies while large are without the specificity of modern words and concepts. Perhaps therein lies the reason that vocables, which might sound meaningless to an outsider, may be able to express rather complex ideas, and may in fact identify and categorize songs for those who use them.[7] Whether words or vocables are used, the more important issue is the purpose and function of the songs, which will now be discussed.

Purpose And Function Of Song And Dance

Native American music and dance do not exist apart from other social and cultural issues. Like African and other musics, it is mostly, if not always, inextricably bound up with all aspects of life and living. Hence there is no performer-audience dichotomy as is found in Western classical music. A major function of music and dance is to clarify the relationship between the natural and the supernatural. This is readily apparent in both the names and the conduct of the many songs and dances. In the same way, reverence for nature and the environment and all the creatures that dwell therein is expressed through song and dance. Song and dance are vehicles for honoring and keeping alive the memory of ancestors. The young learn about their heritage and culture through song and dance. Such virtues as hope, courage, strength, and survival issues are greatly emphasized in song and dance. Of paramount importance to the Native American is underscoring the interconnectedness and interrelationships of life. These ideals are conveyed through various hoop dances, the symbolism of the continuous rings being quite obvious.

A Regional Simulated Field Experience

This experience should help to point out some of the difficulties of cross-cultural studies as well as providing a closer look at a particular indigenous form of expression. A Cherokee Stomp Dance is chosen for this experience, therefore a few words are in order regarding the Cherokee and the Stomp dance as it is practiced among them.

---

6.   Leon L. Bram, Robert S. Phillips,Norma H. Dickey, eds., Funk and Wagnalls New Encyclopedia, Vol. I, (New York: Funk and Wagnalls, Inc., 1975).

7.   Ibid,

The Cherokee are derived from the Hokan-Siouan Stock: The Iroquois Family as indicated previously. A further breakdown of this family is as follows.

Northern Tribes	Southern Tribes	Independents
Six Nations	Cherokee	Huron, or Wyandot
Seneca	Tuscarora	Erie
Cayuga	(before 1715)	Susquehanna, or Conestoga
Onodaga		Neutrals
Oneida Mohawk Tuscarora		
(after 1715)		

This great family was spread through the Appalachian forests of the eastern part of North America. The southern branch, made up of Cherokees or 'cave people" and Tuscaforas or "hemp gatherers," occupied what are now North Carolina and Tennessee. The northerners were scattered in perhaps two hundred different villages from the St. Lawrence River to Ohio and Pennslvania. There is speculation concerning the origin of all the Iroquoian people; some suggest that they migrated from a southern region sometime after the start of the Christian era, and others that they spread southward from near the mouth of the St.Lawrence. Recent evidence, however, indicates that they came from the Mississippi and Ohio River Valleys, and were descendants of mound-buildings of the ancient Midwest.[8]

Now to the Stomp Dance. It appears that the Stomp Dance was part of the Green Corn dance. The Green Corn dance was perhaps of chief importance among Cherokee ceremonials, a custom which has persisted in various forms throughout Cherokee history. Timberlake stated that the dance was performed "in a very solemn manner, in a large square before the town-house door; the motion here is very slow, and the song in which they offer thanks to God for the corn he has sent them, far from unpleasing."[9]

Among ancient Cherokee customs and rites which carried over into the nineteenth century, the Green Corn Dance was most important. By the 1830's it was sometimes rather aptly called the "Stomp Dance," but it was associated with the opening of the green corn season. Fires were kept burning throughout the year for special ceremonial exercises in connection with the festival. [10]

A description of the Stomp dance is found in "Reminiscences of Robert B. Ross, Sr., (grandson of Chief John Ross), copied in "Miscellaneous Letters and Manuscripts," Northeastern, Oklahoma State Teachers College Library, page 114.

---

8.   Alvin M. Josephy, Jr., The Patriot Chiefs. (New York: The VikingPress, 1971), 58.

9.   Henry Thomas Malone, Cherokees of the Old South. (Athens, Georgia: The University of Georgia Press, 1956), 205.

10. Ibid., 206.

The Stomp Dance as a carry-over from the East was described by a Western Cherokee as follows: The full-bloods had their own native religious ceremonies, in the form of stomp-dances. At the... stomp ground they would meet at the time of year when green corn was ready for eating and with the barbecuing of meats and the roasting of the green corn, they would gorge themselves for three days, and on the fourth day they would take their mystical medicines which would cause them to become nauseated and they would vomit, thus cleansing their system and soul of all impurities. They would again start eating and dancing with joy. The womenfolks would attach to their ankles a number of shells in which small rocks were placed and these rock would rattle as they danced and sang, while someone beat on the ... tom-tom. (Interview with W. W. Harnage, I&P Papers, Vol. 39, p. 102-109.)[11]

This description of the Stomp Dance hearkens back to earlier times when more ceremonial significance accompanied the dance. The modern form of the dance recalls its historical significance even as ceremonial aspects have diminished.

An immediate problem in deciphering such dances is that of language. Given the difficulties with respect to languages which were discussed briefly in the beginning of the chapter, it is understandable that the issue surfaces straightaway. Even if one could unravel the language issue, it might not help a great deal, since the songs consist for the most part of vocables or syllables such as *Hey A Ho Way Aye* with very few Cherokee words sparsely interspersed between the vocables. As pointed out earlier, this arrangement of vocables and Cherokee words would perhaps have meaning only to the one who "composed" the song or to those for whom the song was composed. Likewise when one tries to ascertain the form of the songs, it would behoove one not to be too zealous in assigning a definite form. We would do well to remember that those who sang and danced the songs were probably not in the least concerned about any preconceived notion of form. No doubt the form of the song evolved from some direction or necessity inherent in the dance itself or the occasion or purpose for which the song and dance were created. To really understand the form and purpose of the dance, one would probably need to live, communicate directly with, and if possible, participate in such songs and dances. Even then, the real meaning and purpose might be deliberately concealed or simply remain inaccessible due to cultural differences between the hosts and the outsider attempting to do field work.

Melodic issues which present are those of scale, contour, and timbre. The matter of scales was discussed earlier and would obtain even if one were tempted to assign pentatonicism to the melodies heard. Vowel colors and timbrel issues will probably have little relevance to what actually occurs. For lack of better terminology, voice sounds might be described as coarse or hoarse, but then

11. Ibid., 207.

only from a Western point of view. The notion of a percussive concept might be useful as an emphasis on pronounced punctuation might be observed, and punctuation of the most unpredictable sort if subjected to Western notions of accent, stress, arsis, thesis, and so on.

Given the many limitations of any field experience, simulated or otherwise, the two major unconquerable ones would be the limitations of Western notation and the lack of knowledge of the Cherokee tongue. With new knowledge and techniques, one might be able to overcome the latter, while the former would probably forever remain a stumbling block.

Acculturation

As Native Americans were pushed on to the reservations, they sometimes found themselves in close proximity to groups previously unknown to them. This forced proximity led to the inevitable acculturation that occurs while disparate groups are struggling to survive and coexist.

Another clear example of acculturation occurred with some of the Southeastern tribes who lived with, intermarried with, and fought for survival with African slaves and former slaves. These tribes developed unique musical styles quite unlike other Native American groups due to this association. Such characteristics as call-and-response, African vocality, and polyrhythmic proclivities all indicate acculturative processes at work.

Yet another example outside the reservations would be that of the Klingits who exhibit a musical style quite distinct from other Native American groups including a kind of harmony, choral style, and modal sounds which they most likely acquired while trading with the Russians in Alaska.

Two somewhat "religious" examples of acculturation can be seen in the Ghost Dance and the Peyote Cults, cults which are sometimes referred to as the "Native American Church." [12]

The Ghost Dance is a religion that was introduced in the 1880's by tribes further west, in the Great Basin of Nevada; it was a cult outlawed by the U.S.A. in 1891, which preached war and annihilation to the encroaching whites, a last-ditch stand against the inevitable. [13]

The songs associated with the Ghost Dance took on the characteristic styles of those who shared them as they moved from the Great Basin to the Plains.

---

12. Bruno Nettl, Folk and Traditional Music of the Western Continents (New Jersey: Prentice-Hall, 1965), 151.

13. Ibid.

The Peyote religion likewise exhibited acculturative traits as it migrated from group to group. Bruno Nettl describes this unique "Pan-Indian" style of music.

> *Peyote, a cactus indigenous in Mexico, has button which when chewed have a mild narcotic effect, producing euphoria and eventually pleasant hallucinations. The Aztecs already had a cult built around Peyote, but a religion of a different sort, preaching conciliation with the whites and including some superficial elements of Christianity, was based on this drug in North America. Peyote reached some of the Apache tribes after 1700 and spread from them to the majority of tribes in the United States during the nineteenth and early twentieth centuries. The style of Peyote music is essentially the same among all of the North American tribes that use the Peyote ceremonies; and uniformly it differs from the older musical styles of those tribes.[14]*

As seen from this description, Peyote songs embody acculturative traits involving the various groups that use them but also exhibit a kind religious syncretism between native religious practices and Christianity. It also shows that this style of music is probably the most acculturative type in that it eventually spread to a majority of tribes in the United States.

And finally, one last example of acculturation, namely, modern-day **powwows.** Powwows are characteristically intertribal popular events which draw different groups from far and near for celebrations of music, dance, and culture. We are privileged to have such events annually in the writer's hometown in the Quad Cities U.S.A. on the banks of the Mississippi River. At these events we experience native dress, music (singing and drumming), food, cultural artifacts, and occasional weddings and other observances. The greater majority of musical offerings are intertribal. The Plains style of singing seems to predominate but the styles of the many different participating groups are also represented giving vent to a truly acculturative experience.[15]

---

14. Nettl, Folk and Traditional Music of the Western Continents, 151.

15. William Alves, Music of the Peoples of the World. 2n .ed., (Boston, Massachusetts: Schirmer Cengage Learning, 2009) 339.

Powwow
Quad Cities USA
Drummers

Powwow Quad Cities USA

Male Dancer

Powwow - Quad Cities USA
Intertribal Dancers

Powwow - Quad Cities USA

Women Dancers

Young Jingle Dancer

Aesthetics Considerations

Do we really need to talk about aesthetics with respect to native American music and is it even appropriate to do so? The answer has to be a resounding yes, if for no other reason than to point of the vast difference between an aesthetic appropriate to Native American issues and that of other cultures. Obviously one aesthetic does not fit all, nor does a particular aesthetic embody a set of universal truths about anything. At best, a given aesthetic is a particular set of beliefs about a particular system or way of approaching matters, musically or otherwise. Therefore one must tread with extreme caution when broaching the subject of aesthetics pertaining to any particular group. Given the complexities of dealing with such issues with respect to one's own culture, it is a daunting task to approach such issues in cultures so far removed from one's own. Such is the case with Native American culture. With such groups we often encounter a world view we can scarcely image. While the white man was quick to regard indigenous Americans as savages and red devils, the Native American was likewise puzzled by the newcomers as Clark Wissler points out.

> *To his way of thinking, the white man was rude and lacking in good manners. He was selfish and refused to share food, clothing, etc., even when he had an abundance. He scoffed at the most sacred ideas of the Indian and blasphemed the Powers above. True, the Indian respected his power to furnish metal tools, and above all, powder, ball and guns - they were the great magic beyond the power of the Indian to produce. Yet, in the forest, on the trail, the Indian was superior; He taught the white man woodcraft and how to raise corn, beans, squashes and tobacco; how to build and use birchbark canoes, snowshoes and the toboggan and play lacrosse. The medicine men taught him their formulas for the use of plants and many other beliefs respecting luck and health, thereby enriching colonial folklore. [16]*

The difference in world view is profound and is further pointed out by Wissler.

> *It was a different world the Indian lived in. We spend our time on paved roads and cross streams on bridges. We have cleared away the forests, dried up the swamps and destroyed much of the interesting wildlife of the country.*

> *Much of the native flora has been swept away to make room for crops, meadows and golf courses. Surrounding ourselves by all sorts of mechanical aids, we have forgotten nature as the Indian knew it. He was at home in the forest; we are afraid. So much of our world is manmade that we think in terms of mechanics, a world which we*

---

16. Clark Wissler, <u>Indians of the United States</u>, (Garden City, New York: Doubleday & Company, Inc, 1966),.

manipulate and control. With the Indian it was different. He saw living creatures on every hand; he spied upon them until he knew their ways; he marveled at their skill in alluding him, their humanlike ways and his inability to communicate with them. He felt the forest as a living thing; the trees were to him almost as persons, and the winds were the breath of some great unseen supernatural. When the storm clouds rolled, the thunder pealed, the tornado crashed through the trees, he felt the powers upon the highest level of creative and destructive force. As he walked abroad, he felt himself in the presence of living things conscious of his existence, who could speak to him, if they chose, and at any time change his fortunes for good or ill. To them he turned for guidance and wisdom.[17]

In other words the Native American seeks to be at one with nature, not to fully understand it or to subdue or conquer it. While fearing the supernatural and humbling himself before the same, he at the same expresses utmost confidence in it. Views concerning things natural and supernatural might seem incomprehensible to an outsider, leading as it often did to disparate views between the newcomers and their Native American hosts.

These diametrically opposed views often made it impossible for outsiders to understand and appreciate the values of their hosts, such as the profound dignity, graceful movements, formality, and even silence that accompanied the dances and other ceremonials. While the meticulous execution of these values was a matter of showing respect and veneration by the insiders, the newcomers were bored, impatient, and unappreciative.

Hopi Dwellings

---

17. Wissler, <u>Indians of the United States,</u> 304-305.

Bruno Nettl points out the difference between the typical Western aesthetic and one that is more appropriate to the Native American.

a) The mark of a good singer on the Plains is the ability to sing many songs, and to sing high.

b) The Pueblo prefer singers with low, growling voices.

c) Songs are judged according their power rather their "beauty." [18]

These three brief references are miniscule when faced with the many other considerations one encounters when approaching the matter of aesthetics cross-culturally.

18. Nettl, Folk and Traditional Music of the Western Continents. 152.

NATIVE AMERICAN VISION STATEMENT
As First Americans,
we walk in the present,
with our eyes on the future
and the past in our hearts.

We advocate pride
in our cultural integrity.
We honor the spirit
that ensures continuity
of the sacred circle.

Source Unknown

Native American Musical Instruments

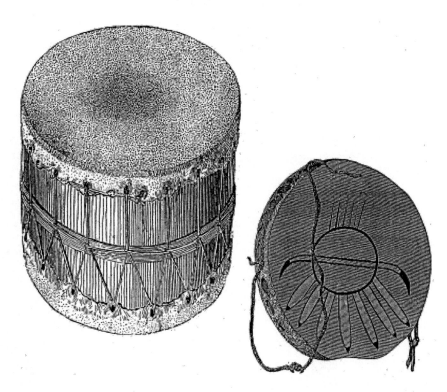

Drums
(Membranophones)

Drumstick
(Navajo and Apache)

Rattles (Idiophones)

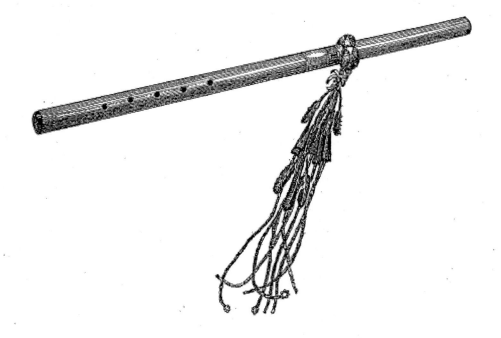

Flute
(Aerophone)

Rasp
(Scraped Idiophone)

Chapter Reference

Preface

Malm, William P. "Music as a Non-International Universal," Quarterly Journal. Vol. 3, No. 4, December, 1974,35.

Chapter 1

Kartomi, Margaret J. On Concepts and Classifications of Musical Instruments. Chicago: University of Chicago Press, 1990.

Reck David. Music of the Whole Earth. New York: Charles Scribner's Sons, 1977.

Sachs, Curt and Erich M. von Hornbostel. "Classification of Musical Instruments," Systematik der Musikinstrumente. trans. Anthony Baines and Klaus P. Wachsmann, Zeitschrift fur Ethnology. Jahrg., 1914, Heft 4 u.5 (Berlin, 1914).

Van Aalst, J. A. Chindese Music. New York: Paragon Book Reprint Corporation, 1966.

Chapter 2

Alves, William. Music of the Peoples of the World. Belmont, California: Thomson-Schirmer, 2006.

Blackwood, Alan. "Music in the Bible," Music of the World. Englewood Cliffs, New Jersey: Prentice-Hall, Inc., 1991.

Desto Records. (Record Jacket Notes), "The Arab World, Its Music and Its People." (Desto Album I) 504,1969.

Duvelle, Charles. African Music (Papers read at a meeting organized by UNESCO in Yaounde, Cameroon, 23-27 February 1970). 7 Place Saint Sulpice, Paris: La Revue Musicale, 1972.

Harris, William H. and Judith S. Levey. The New Columbia Encyclopedia. New York: Columbia University Press, 1975.

Hoffer, Charles. Music Listening Today. (3rd ed.). Belmont, California: Thomson-Schirmer, 2007.

Malm, William P. Music Cultures of the Pacific, Near East and Asia (3rd.ed). Upper Saddle River, New Jersey: Prentice-Hall, 1996.

NettLBruno, Excursions in World Music. Upper Saddle River, New Jersey: Prentice-Hall, 2008.

Nketia, J.H.K. The Music of Africa (Papers read at a meeting organized by UNESCO in Yaounde, Cameroon, 23-27 February, 1970), (7 Place Saint Sulpice, Paris: "La Revue Musicale," 1972.

Oriental Music Festival. Elvet Hill, Durham, England: School of Oriental Studies, 1983.

Slobin, Mark. "Afghanistan," The New Grove Dictionary of Music and Musicians, ed. Stanley Sadie. New York: McMillan Publishers, Ltd., 1980.

Chapter 3

Butcher, Vada E. Development of Materials for a One Year Course in African Music for the General Graduate Student (Final Report) Washington, D.C.: U. S. Department of Health, Education, and Welfare, 1970.

Duvelle, Charles. "Oriental Music in Black Africa," African Music. Paris: La Revue Musicale, 1970.

Hornbostel, Erich M. von. "African Negro Music," Africa. I/I, 1928.

Jones, A. M. "The Homogeneity of African Music," Studies in African Music. 1959.

Merriam, Alan. African Music, Continuity and Change in African Culture. ed. William R. Bascom and Melville J. Herskovits. Chicago: University of Chicago Press, 1959.

Merriam, Alan. Africa "South" of the Sahara (Booklet notes for the record album of the same title). New York: Folkways Records, 1957.

Merriam. Alan P. "Characteristics of African Music." International Folk Music Journal. 1959.

Opoku, A. M. "Thoughts From the School of Music and Drama Institute of African Studies," Okyeame. II/I. Legon, Ghana: University of Ghana, 1964.

Wachsmann, Klaus P. "The Interrelations of Musical Instruments, Musical Forms, and Cultural Systems in Africa," Technology and Culture. v/12,1971.

Waterman, Richard A. "'Hot Rhythm in Negro Music," Journal of the American Musicological Society. I/I, 1948.

Chapter 4

Blackwood, Alan. Music of the World. Englewood Cliffs, New Jersey: Prentice-Hall, Incorporated, 1991.

Funk and Wagnails New International Dictionary of the English Language. Chicago,Illinois: Ferguson Publishing Company, 2001.

Hall, Fernau. "Indian Dance," <u>Oriental Music Festival</u>. Elvet Hill, Durham, England: School of Oriental Studies, 1983.

Malm, William P. <u>Music Cultures of the Pacific, the Near East and Asia.</u> Engelwood Cliffs, New Jersey: Prentice-Hall. Inc., 1967.

Neuman, Daniel M. The Life <u>of Music in North India.</u> Chicago, Illinois: University of Chicago Press, 1990.

Panda, Ruchira. "Indian Classical Music: An Overview." Unpublished.

Chapter 5

Blackwood, Alan. <u>Music of the World</u>. Englewood Cliffs, New Jersey: Prentice-Hall, Incorporated, 1991.

<u>JVC Video Anthology of World Music and Dance.</u> Pakistan."Montpelier, Vermont: Rounder Records, 1991.

Qureshi, Regula. "Pakistan," <u>New Grove's Dictionary of Music and Musicians.</u> Vol 14, Stanley Sadie, ed. London: Macmillan, 1980.

Chapter 6

Anonymous. "Chinese Music." Taipei, Taiwan: China Publishing Co., 1977.

Harris, William H. and Judith S. Levey, eds. "China," <u>The New Columbia Encyclopedia.</u> New York: Columbia University Press, 1975.

Nettl, Bruno, et. al. <u>Excursions in World Music</u>. Englewood Cliffs, New Jersey: Prentice Hall, 1992.

Van Aalst, J. A. <u>Chinese Music.</u> New York: Paragon Book Reprint Corporation, 1966.

Chapter 7

Alves,Wiliam. <u>Music of the Peoples of the World.</u> Belmont. California: Thomson-Schirmer, 2006.

Malm, William P. <u>Music Cultures of the Pacific, the Near East, and Asia.</u> Upper Saddle River, New Jersey: Prentice-Hall, Inc., 1966.

Chapter 8

Alves, William, <u>Music of the Peoples of the World. Belmont California:</u> Thomson-Schirmer, 2006.

Fujie, Linda, "East Asia/Japan," <u>Worlds of Music: An Introduction to the Music of the World's Peoples,</u> 4th ed., Jeff Todd Titon, ed. Belmont, CA: Schirmer-Thomson, 2002.

Harris, William H., and Judith S. Levey, eds., <u>The New Columbia Encyclopedia.</u> New York: Columbia University Press, 1975.

Kishibe, Shigeo, <u>Traditional Music of Japan</u> (Record Jacket Notes) [Victor Records JL-32-4J.

Malm, William P., "Japan," <u>New Grove's Dictionary of Music and Musicians,</u> Stanley Sadie, ed. NewYork: McMillan Publishers, Ltd., 1980.

Malm, William P., <u>Japanese Music and Musical Instruments.</u> Rutland, Vermont: Charles E. Turtle Company, 1973.

Malm, William P., <u>Music Cultures of the Pacific, the Near East, and Asia.</u> Upper Saddle River, New Jersey: Prentice-Hall, Inc., 1996.

Malm, William P., <u>Nagauta.</u> Westpoint, Connecticut: Greenwood Press Publishers, 1973.

O'Brien, James P., <u>Non-Western Music and the Western Listener.</u> Dubuque, Iowa: Kendall/Hunt Publishing Co., 1977.

<u>Oriental Music Festival.</u> Elvet Hill, Durham, England: School of Oriental Studies, 1983.

Wong, Isabel, "The Music of Japan," <u>Excursions in World Music,</u> Bruno Nettl, et. al. Upper Saddle River, New Jersey, 2008.

Chapter 9

Harris, William H. and Judith S. Levey, <u>The New Columbia Encyclopedia.</u> New York: Columbia University Press, 1975.

Lee, Byong Won, "Korea," <u>New Grove's Dictionary of Music and Musicians.</u> Stanley Sadie, ed. London: Macmillan, 1980.

Malm, William P., <u>Music Cultures of the Pacific. Near East, and Asia.</u> Upper Saddle River, New Jersey: Prentice-Hall, Inc., 1996.

Van Aalst, J. A., <u>Chinese Music.</u> New York: Paragon Book Reprint Corp., 1966.

Chapter 10

Alves, William, <u>Music of the Peoples of the World.</u> (2nd ed.) Boston, Massachusetts: Schirmer Cengage Learning, 2009.

Holt, Claire, <u>Art in Indonesia.</u> New York: Cornell University Press, 1967.

Hood, Mantle and Hardja Susilo, <u>Music of the Venerable Dark Cloud: the Javanese Gamelan Khjai Mendung.</u> Los Angeles, CA: UCLA Institute of Ethnomusicology, 1967.

<u>JVC Video Anthology of World Music and Dance,</u> "Southeast Asia." (Indonesia 2, Tape 10.) Montpelier, Vermont: New England Networks, 1991.

Larsen, Arved M., <u>Crossroads in Music.</u> Belmont, California: Thomson-Schirmer, 2003.

Malm, William P., <u>Music Cultures of the Pacific, the Near East, and Asia.</u> Upper Saddle River, New Jersey: Prentice-Hall, Inc., 1996.

McPhee, Colin, <u>Music in Bali.</u> New York: Da Capo, 1976.

Morgan, Stephanie and Laurie J. Sears, eds., <u>Aesthetic Tradition and Cultural Transition in Java and Bali.</u> Madison, Wisconsin: Center for Southeast Asian Studies -University of Wisconsin, 1984.

Nettl, Bruno, et. al, <u>Excursions in World Music.</u> Upper Saddle River, New Jersey: Pearson/Prentice-Hall, 2004.

O'Brien, James P., <u>Non-Western Music and the Western Listener.</u> Dubuque, Iowa: Kendall/Hunt Publishing Company, 1977.

Chapter 11

Alves, William, <u>Music of the Peoples of the World.</u> Belmont, California: Thomson-Schirmer, 2006.

Blackwood, Alan, <u>Music of the World.</u> Englewood Cliffs, New Jersey: Prentice-Hall Incorporated, 1991.

Carew, Jan, "African-American Studies - A Position Paper," (unpublished manuscript). Evanston, Illinois: Northwestern University, 1972.

Carew, Jan, The Origins of Racism in America," (unpublished manuscript). Evanston, Illinois: Northwestern University, n.d..

Courlander, Harold, "African and Afro-American Drums," <u>Ethnic Folkways Library.</u> New York: Folkways Records and Service Corporation, 1962.

Nettl, Bruno, et. al., <u>Excursions in World Music.</u> Upper Saddle River, New Jersey: Pearson-Prentice Hall, 2008.

Nettl, Bruno, <u>Folk and Traditional Music of the Western Continents.</u> New Jersey: Prentice-Hall, 1965.

Rondel, Don, "Flamenco," <u>Harvard Dictionary of Music.</u> Cambridge, Mass.: Harvard University Press, 1986.

Van Sertima, Ivan, "African Folk Archetypes in the New World," (unpublished paper). Evanston, Illinois, n.d..

Waterman, Richard Alan, "On Flogging a Dead Horse: Lessons Learned from the Africanisms Controversy," <u>Journal of Ethnomusicology,</u> VII/2, May, 1963.

Chapter 12

Alves, William, <u>Music of the Peoples of the World,</u> 2nd . ed. Boston, Massachusetts: Schirmef-Cengage Learning, 2009.

Bram, Leon L., Robert S. Phillips, and Norma H. Dickey, eds., "American Indians," <u>Funk and Wagnalls New Encyclopedia,</u> Vol 1. New York: Funk and Wagnalls, Inc., 1975.

Desmnore, Frances, "Scale in Indian Music," <u>The American Indians and Their Music.</u> New York: The Woman's Press, 1926.

Harris, William H. and Judith S. Levey, eds., <u>The New Columbia Encyclopedia.</u> New York: Columbia University Press, 1975.

Josephy, AlvinM., <u>The Patriot Chiefs.</u> New York: The Viking Press, 1971.

Malone, Henry Thomas, <u>Cherokees of the Old South.</u> Athens, Georgia: The University Of Georgia Press, 1956.

Nettl, Bruno, <u>Folk and Traditional Music of the Western Continents.</u> New Jersey: Prentice-Hall, 1965.

Nettl, Bruno, "North American Indian Musical Styles," <u>The American Folklore Society,</u> 1954.

Wissler, Clark, <u>Indians of the United States</u>. Garden City, New York: Doubleday and Company, Inc., 1966.

General Bibliography

Bakan, Michael B. World Music: Traditions and Transformations. New York: McGraw-Hill Companies, Inc., 2007.

Behague, Gerard. Music in Latin America: An Introduction. Englewood Cliffs, New Jersey:'Prentice-Hall, 1979.

Bohlman, Philip V. World Music: A Very Short Introduction. New York: Oxford Press, 2002.

Broughton, Simon, et. al., eds. World Music: The Rough Guide. London: The Rough Guides, 2000.

Diamond, Beverly. Native American Music in Eastern North America. New York: Oxford University Press, 2008.

Hamm, Charles, Bruno Nettl, and Ronald Byrnside. Contemporary Music and Music Cultures. Englewood Cliffs, New Jersey: Prentice-Hall, Inc., 1975.

Kaemmer, John E. Music in Human Life: Anthropological Perspectives on Music. Austin, Texas: University of Texas Press, 1993.

Manuel, Peter. Popular Music of the Non-Western World. New York: Oxford University Press, 1988.

Marcuse, Sibyl. Musical Instruments: A Comprehensive Dictionary. New York: W. W. Norton and Co., Inc., 1975.

May Elizabeth, ed. Musics of Many Cultures. Berkeley, California: University of California Press, 1980.

Morgan, Stephanie and Laurie Jo Sears, eds. Aesthetic Tradition and Cultural Transition in Java and Bali. Madison, Wisconsin: Center For Southeast Asian Studies, 1984.

Nettl, Bruno. Music In Primitive Culture. Cambridge, Mass.: Harvard University Press, 1956.

Nettl, Bruno. The Study of Ethnomusicology: Thirty-One Issues and Concepts. Urbana, Illinois: University of Illinois Press, 2005.

Nettl, Bruno. The Western Impact on World Music: Change. Adaptation and Survival. New York: Schirmer Books, 1985.

Porter, James and Timothy Rice, eds. The Garland Encyclopedia of World Music. New York: Garland, 1998.

Randel, Don, ed. The New Harvard Dictionary of Music. Cambridge, Mass: The Belknap Press of Harvard University Press, 1986.

Reck, David. <u>Music of the Whole Earth.</u> New York: Charles Scribner's Sons, 1977.

Sadie, Stanley. <u>The New Grove Dictionary of Music and Musicians.</u> New York: Macmillan Publishers Limited, 1980.

Shelemay, Kay Kaufman. <u>Soundscapes: Exploring Music in a Changing World.</u> New York: W. W. Norton and Company, 2001.

Stevenson, Robert. <u>Music in Mexico.</u> New York: Thomas Y. Crowell Company, 1952.

Titon, Jeff Todd. <u>World's of Music: An Introduction to the Music of theWorld's Peoples.</u> 3rd. ed. Belmont, California: Schirmer Cengage Learning, 2009.

Waterman, Christopher Alan. <u>Juju: A Social History and Ethnography of an African Popular Music</u>. Chicago: University of Chicago Press, 1990.

Westrup, J. A. and F. Ll. Harrison. <u>The New College Encyclopedia of Music.</u> New York: W. W. Norton and Co., 1976.

White, Gary, David Stuart, and Elyn Aviva. <u>Music In Our World.</u> New York: McGraw-Hill Companies, Inc., 2001.

Glossary

Abhinaya: Indian dance interpretation using gestures.

Acoustic: An instrument that is not amplified.

Acoustics: The science of sound.

Aerophones: Instruments that produce their sounds through a vibrating column of air in a tube or pipe, a wind instrument.

Africanisms: Identifiable African characteristics in music.

Ageng: Large in size (gong ageng, a large gong).

Agogo: West African double bell (and Brazil).

Akadinda: An large African xylophone with twenty-two keys.

Akan: A West African ethnic group in Ghana.

Alap: Introductory, exploratory part of a raga.

Amplitude: The loudness or softness of sound caused by the amount of force exerted on a vibrating medium.

Angklung: An Indonesian pitched bamboo rattle, a shaken idiophone.

Anupallavi: The second section in a kriti or South Indian song.

Apache Fiddle: A bowed, one-string fiddle used by the Navajo and Apache people.

Arja: Balinese opera (Indonesia).

Atsimevu: A large, lead drum in West Africa used by the Ewe people.

Atumpan: A pair of large drums used by the Akan people of Ghana.

Avaz: A central section that is nonmetric and improvised in Persian classical music.

Axatse: A shaken idiophone with a beaded net stretched over a gourd used by the Ewe people.

Aymara: A large ethnic group in the Andes.

Bansuri: A Hindustani flute.

Bantu: A major African language group.

Barong: A trance dance in Indonesia. Also a lion-like mythical creature.

Baya:　　　　　　　　　The smaller drum of the tqbla pair in india.

Bedhaya:　　　　　　　Javanese sacred court dance.

Beshrav:　　　　　　　A metrical, introductory piece in Turkish classical music.

Bin:　　　　　　　　　A Hindustani plucked lute.

Biwa:　　　　　　　　A Japanese, pear-shaped plucked lute.

Bonang:　　　　　　　An elaboration instrument in the Javanese gamelan.

Bongo:　　　　　　　A single-headed pair of drums in Latin America.

Buddhism:　　　　　　A religion based on the teachings of Buddha.

Bugaku:　　　　　　　Instrumentally accompanied Japanese court dance.

Bunraku:　　　　　　Japanese puppet theater.

Candomble:　　　　　A West African-derived Afro-Brazilian religion.

Call-and-response:　　Alternation back and forth between different voices or Instruments.

Cantor:　　　　　　　A lead singer in Jewish religious services.

Caranum:　　　　　　The third and last section in the kriti of South India.

Carnatic:　　　　　　South India (also Karnatak).

Cha-Cha-Cha:　　　　A dance-music genre from Cuba.

Chahar mezrab:　　　A Persian classical music piece which is composed, metric, and virtuosic.

Charango:　　　　　A small Andean guitar sometimes made from the shell of an armadillo.

Chassidism:　　　　Judaism that developed in the 18th century in Eastern and Central Europe.

Chinese Communist Party:　The People's Republic of China led originally by Mao Zedong Established in 1949.

Chobo:　　　　　　Kabuki stage duo called the Gidayu.

Chord:　　　　　　A group of three or more tones sounding simultaneously.

Chord progression:　The process of moving from one chord to another.

Chordophones:　　Stringed instruments that produce their sounds through the agency of tightly-stretched strings.

Confucianism:　　The philosophical and socio-political teachings of Confucius (551-479 B.C.E.).

Conga:	West African-derived Afro-Cuban drums, large and barrel-shaped.
Conjunto:	Latin American popular dance music found along the Mexico-Texas border.
Copla:	A Latin American verse form derived from Portugal.
Criollo:	American-born or European-derived groups in Latin America.
Cuture:	Everything that characterizes or describes a particular social entity.
Dan:	Section, part, etude.
Dangdut:	A popular song type in Indonesia which is homiletic, Islamic in orientation, and influencedby Hindu film music.
Danzon:	National dance of Cuba.
Darbucca:	A characteristic goblet-shaped drum found throughout the Middle East.
Dastgah:	Scalar-modal formulas found in Persian classical music.
Debayashi:	Kabuki on-stage musicians.
Decrescendo:	Becoming gradually softer.
Dhalang:	Puppeteer of the Indonesian shadow puppet theater.
Dhrupad:	Instrumental and song form of North India.
Diaspora:	Those who have been dispersed from their original homeland.
Diatonic:	The Western seven-note scale.
Dizi:	A Chinese bamboo flute with six finger holes.
Drone:	A sustained, continuous sound.
Dundun:	An African talking drum (hourglass-shaped).
Duration:	The length of the vibration producing a tone.
Dynamic range:	Levels of loudness and softness in musical sounds.
Electronophones:	Instruments that produce their sounds through electronic means.
Ensemble:	Groups of combined instruments or voices.
Erhu:	A spike fiddle from China with two strings.
Erhuang:	A type of aria in Peking Opera.

Ethnocentrism:	Concentration on one particular ethnic focus or perspective.
Ethnomusicology:	The global study of music in its social and cultural context.
Fieldwork:	On-sight observation and study of music and culture, the hallmark of ethnomusicology and anthropology.
Filmgit:	Indian film songs.
Flat:	A tone lowered by a half step.
Form:	The design and shape of music.
Free rhythm:	Music lacking a discernible meter or beat pattern.
Frequency:	The speed of vibrations which governs the highness or lowness of a particular pitch.
Fret:	A fingerboard device that allows the player to stop the strings in order to achieve the desired pitch.
Fushi:	A term for melody in Japanese music.
Gagaku:	Japanese court music.
Gambang:	Javanese xylophone-like instrument.
Gamelan:	Generic term for orchestra or ensemble in Indonesia.
Gat:	The part of a Hindustani performance following the alap or introductory section, characterized by a pulse and governed by a tala.
Geza:	The Kabuki off-stage music ensemble.
Ghazal:	A form of poetry sung in North India and Pakistan by speakers of Urdu and is associated with Persian, Arabic, and Muslim culture.
Ghost Dance:	A Native American movement that was outlawed by the U. S. government because of its strenuous protests against U.S. government actions towards Native Americans.
Gidayubushi:	A Japanese shamisen-accompanied narrative style.
Gong:	An Indonesian oval idiophone that vibrates when struck.
Gong ageng:	The largest of the large gongs usually responsible for indicating the beginning of the recurring cycle in the colotomic structure.
Griot:	A hereditary class of musicians responsible for designated songs and music traditions, a bard.
Guru:	A teacher, mentor, spiritual advisor in Indian traition.

Hako:	A Pawnee (Native American) ceremony consisting of four days of singing, dancing, and ritual.
Halam:	A West African banjo-like chordophone.
Hanamichi:	A Kabuki theater ramp that connects the stage to the back of the theater along which actors enter and exit.
Harmonium:	A small hand-pumped organ introduced to North and South India by missionaries.
Harmony:	A vertical arrangement of notes accompanying melody.
Hayashi:	Japanese drum and flute ensembles.
Heterophony:	The simultaneous rendering of the same melody by two or more participants.
Hexatonic:	A six-note scale.
Hichiriki:	A Japanese oboe, a double-reed aerophone.
Hindustani:	North Indian musical style.
Hocket:	A melody created by interlocking parts from different sources.
Hogaku:	Japanese music.
Holocaust:	The systematic murder of six million Jews and others by the Nazis in World War II.
Hornbostel-Sachs:	The creators of an internationally recognized system for classifying musical instruments worldwide.
Iberian:	The Iberian Peninsula, Spain and Portugal.
Idiophone:	An instrument whose own sonorous material is caused to vibrate without the aid of strings, membranes, wind, or any other extraneous materials, a self-sounding instrument.
Improvisation:	Spontaneous creation or performance of music.
Interlocking:	See hocket style.
Instrumentation:	The designation of instruments (and voices) to be used in a musical performance.
Interval:	The distance between two pitches.
Jali:	A professional musician in parts of Africa (see griot).
Jewish Diaspora:	Jews who have been dispersed from their original homeland.

Jhala:	The final section in a Hindustani performance which follows the jor section and is characterized by very fast and lively rhythmic passages.
Jiangnan sizhu:	A Chinese instrumental chamber ensemble consisting of string and wind instruments.
Jianzipu:	Tablature for the qin, a seven-stringed Chinese zither.
Kabuki:	The popular music theater of Japan.
Kagura-bue:	A Japanese flute used in court and Shinto music.
Kakko:	A small Japanese, horizontal drum used in court music.
Kamancheh:	A Middle eastern chordophone, a spiked fiddle of three to four strings and played with a horsehair bow.
Karnatak:	South Indian style of music.
Kebyar: Kecak:	
Kathak:	Principal style of Hindustani dance (North India).Modern Balinese music and dance.
	Balinese "monkey chant" in which chattering human voices imitate the sounds and intricate workings of the gamelan.
Keeping Tala:	Marking the beats of the tala with a pattern of claps, waves, and finger movements.
Kempul:	A small suspended gong that participates in the colotomic structure of the Javanese gamelan.
Kena:	An ancient Andean flute.
Kenong:	A large horizontal gong that participates in the colotomic structure.
Kethuk:	A small Javanese gong that functions colotomically.
Key:	The major or minor scale on which the music is based.
Khyak:	Major vocal style of Hindustani music.
Kidi:	A middle-sized drum used for accompanying by the Ewe people.
Klezmer:	A modern Jewish instrumental ensemble.
Koma-bue:	A Japanese court music flute.
Koma-gaku:	Japanese court music from Korea.
Kora:	A harp-lute with twenty-one strings played by the Jali.

Koran: The Sacred Book of Islam.

Koto: A Japanese zither with thirteen strings and moveable bridges.

Ko-tsuzumi: A small hourglass-shaped drum of Japan.

Kriti: A Karnatak principal song type.

Kroncong: Portuguese-influenced popular music of Indonesia.

Kushaura: In Shona Mbira music, the lead part or first part, meaning literally "to lead the piece."

Kutsinhira: The second accompanying part in Shona mbira music.

Lamellaphone: A thumb piano, played by striking metal or reed tongues.

Laras: The tuning system in Javanese music.

Legato: Smoothly, sustained, connected.

Lute: A stringed instrument with strings traveling down a neck to the sound box.

Mahour: A mode in Persian music, one of twelve.

Major: A western scale consisting of a series of whole-steps and half-steps with a half-step between the third and fourth degree and the seventh and eighth degree.

Mambo: A Latin dance rhythm

Makam: A Middle Eastern mode, the Turkish spelling of maqam.

Mao Zedong: Leader of the Chinese Communist oparty from 1949 until 1976.

Maqam: Term for mode used throughout the Middle East with various spellings.

Mariachi: Originally a Mexican ensemble consisting of violins, guitars, and trumpets.

May Fourth Movement: A demonstration by students in Tianamen Square on May 4,1919 protesting the Treaty of Versailles.

Mbira: A thumb piano of the Shona people.

Melevi: A Sufi mystical order in Turkey.

Measure: Metrical units in music.

Melody: The horizontal entity in music.

Membranophones:	Instruments which produce their sounds through the agency of a tightly-stretched skin or membrane.
Mestizo:	The fusion of Native-American and European cultures.
Metallophone:	An idiophone made of metal.
Meter:	The method of measuring or organizing music into metrical units.
Microtones:	Pitch intervals smaller than the Western half-step.
Minor:	A Western scale with half-steps between the second and third degrees and the fifth and sixth degrees.
Mode:	The manner of arranging a series of tones which serve as the basis of music making.
Modulation:	Moving from one key or mode to another in a musical piece.
Monophonic:	Music consisting of a single layer or melody without any vertical accompaniment, chords, or harmony.
Motreb:	Generic designation for musicians throughout the Middle East region.
Mridangam:	The characteristic barrel-shaped, double-headed drum of the South Indian Karnatak tradition.
Mugam:	The Azerbaijan spelling for the term maqam.
Musical Bow:	A monochord or bent stick with one string and sometimes with a gourd resonator.
Musical syncretism:	The fusion of different musical systems into new polyethnic products.
Nada Brahma:	Literally "the Sound of God" which is thought to be the divine source of all sound and thus all music as well.
Nagasvaram:	A Karnatak double-reed aerophone or oboe.
Nagauta:	A genre of shamisen music lyrically rendered.
Nationalistic music:	Music that emphasizes national identity.
Natural:	A sign indicating that a pitch is neither lowered nor raised from its original state.
Nay:	A middle Eastern end-blown flute.
Noh:	The classical drama of Japan.
Nohkan:	The Noh flute.

Notation:	A visual representation of music through the use of symbols.
O-tsuzumi:	A larger version of the ko-tsuzumi, an hour-glass shaped drum of Japan.
Octave:	Higher and lower versions of the same pitch name, eight pitches apart.
Organology:	The study and classification of musical instruments worldwide.
Ornamentation:	The addition of ornamental figures and notes in order to embellish a melody.
Orquesta:	Latin American term for orchestra.
Ostinato:	A melodic and/or rhythmic pattern that is repeated stubbornly or incessantly.
Oud (Ude,Ud):	A common pear-shaped Middle Eastern lute.
Pachamama:	The Andean concept of "Earthmother," the living, spiritual earth.
Pallavi:	The introductory section of a Karnatak song.
Pathet:	A particular form or mode of a scale in Java.
Peking Opera:	The principal type of popular Chinese musical theater.
Pelog:	A heptatonic scale in Javanese music.
Pentatonic:	A scale with five pitches.
Peyote Music:	The music associated with the Peyote Cult whose practitioners use a drug from a cactus which is a mild hallucinogen.
Pipa:	A four-stringed, pear-shaped lute of China.
Pishdaramad:	The introductory section in Persian classical music played by an ensemble and is metric and composed.
Polphonic:	Two or more lines or layers of music.
Polyrhythm:	Two or more rhythmic patterns occurring simultaneously.
Powwow:	A Native American tribal or intertribal gathering celebrating music, dance, and culture.
Praise Songs:	A type of song sung to honor royalty, politicians, or patrons.
Qanuni:	A plucked dulcimer from the MiddleEast.
Qin:	Chinese zither, a seven-stringed chordophone.

Quarter note:	A note division in Western music equaling one beat.
Quechua:	The principal Andean language, the language of the incas.
Quran:	The sacred book of Islam.
Quarter tone:	A microtone halfway between the Western half-step.
Rabbinic Judaism:	Judaism dating from the Roman Empire.
Rabbis:	Specialists and leaders in matters of Jewish religion and tradition.
Radif:	A repertoire or set of pieces studied and learned as part of musicianship training in Persian classical music.
Raga:	The scalar-melodic framework that is the basis of musical creation and performance.
Ranchera:	A type of Mexican song associated with working-class and rural people.
Rasa:	The affection or color associated with a particular raga.
Rebab:	A Javanese bowed lute.
Reform Judaism:	A modern form of Judaism that recognizes the need to change with the times and social conditions.
Reng:	The final piece in a performance of Persian Classical music.
Reyong:	Small hand-held gongs in a set of four played by four separate Performers in an interlocking style.
Rhythm:	The element of movement and motion in music.
Riffs:	Short melodic or rhythmic patters repeated in ostinato fashion.
Riqq:	An Arabic tambourine.
Ritsu:	A principal Japanese scale.
Rumba:	An Afro-Cuban dance rhythm.
Ryo:	Another basic Japanese scale (see Ritsu).
Ryuteki:	The characteristic flute used in Gagaku.
Salsa:	The generic term for Latin dance music in and around New York.
Sam:	In the tala cycle, the first beat.
Samba:	A principal Brazilian genre and rhythm.

Samurai:	Japanese warrior.
Sanghyang:	Spirit possession in Balinese and Javanese trance dances.
Sangita:	Music and performing arts in India.
Sankyoku:	A type of music played by a trio in Japan.
Santeria:	Syncretistic religious practices drawing on Afro-Cuban and West African rituals.
Santour:	A middle Eastern hammered dulcimer.
Santur:	The hammered dulcimer of India.
Sarod:	A plucked Hindustani chordophone resembling the sitar.
Saron:	A resonated xylophone-like instrument of Indonesia.
Scale:	A series of pitches in ascending and descending order.
Sesquialtera:	The combining of duple and triple meters in the same or different instrumental parts.
Setar:	A Persian classical, four-stringed, long-necked lute.
Shanameh:	The National Epic (pre-Islamic of Iran.
Shakuhachi:	A Japanese, end-blown bamboo flute.
Shamisen:	A three-stringed banjo-like plucked chordophone of Japan.
Sharp:	A sign indicating that a pitch is raised one half-step from its original point.
Shashmakom:	Literally "six makams" in Central Asia and is comparable to the Persian radif and the Middle Eastern system of maqams.
Shenai:	Indian oboe, double-reed aerophone.
Sheng:	Chinese mouth organ.
Shinto:	Literally "the way of the gods," the native religion of Japan.
Shite:	The principal actor in the Noh drama.
Sho:	A free-reed mouth organ, descended from the Chinese Sheng..
Shoko:	A bronze gagaku drum.
Shomyo:	Buddhist chanting of Japan.
Shur:	A major mode of the Persian classical music system.
Siku:	A double row of panpipes found in the Andes.

Sitar:	A large Hindustani plucked chordophone with three sets of strings.
Sixteenth notes:	A subdivision in Western meter equaling one fourth of the quarter note.
Slendro:	The pentatonic scale of Java.
Society:	A group of people bound together by its own beliefs, customs, and traditions.
Sokyoku:	Japanese koto music.
Son:	An Afro-Cuban and Mexican dance music style.
Songs for the Masses:	Political songs used by the Chinese Communists.
Sruti:	A small microtone within the Indian scalar compass.
Staccato:	To execute a note in a short, detached manner.
Strophic form:	The same music is repeated again and again with different text for each stanza.
Sufism:	A mystical movement of Islam found throughout the Middle East.
Suling:	A vertical flute of Indonesia.
Suona:	A Chinese oboe, double-reed aerophone.
Suya:	A primitive, Amazonian group in Brazil.
Synagogue:	A Jewish house of worship, instruction, and observances.
Syncopation:	An altering of the customary stress patterns in music.
Tabla:	A pair of drums of North India.
Taiko"	A type of drum used in Japanese Noh drama. Also used Generically.
Takht:	An Arabic ensemble of musicians.
Tala:	The rhythmic mode or formula used in Indian music.
Tambura:	A long-necked lute used to play the drone in Indian music.
Tanam:	The section following the alapanam or introduction in Karnatak that introduces a pulse.
Taqsim:	An instrumental piece with several short sections improvised non-metrically in the Arabic and Turkish tradition.
Tar:	A long-necked lute found throughout the Middle East.
Tasnif:	A composed, metric song in Persian music.

Tempo:	Velocity or rate of speed in music.
Texture:	The manner of combinations and relationships in a musical fabric.
Thumri:	A Hindustani instrumental and song style.
Timbales:	A Latin drum set.
Timbre:	The tone color or quality of sound.
Tintal:	A tala of 16 beats.
Togaku:	Japanese gagaku music which came from China and India.
Tonal languages:	Languages that are governed by pitch and rhythms in rendering their meanings.
Tonic:	
Torah:	The keynote or first pitch of a scale, the central pitch or focal point of a given scale.
	The heart of the Hebrew Scriptures.
Triadic harmony:	Vertical sonorities in the European tradition consisting of three pitches a third apart.
Tritone:	An augmented fourth or diminished fifth in European terms which was considered so harsh as to be associated with the devil (the diabolus in musica).
Tsuri-daiko:	A suspended gagaku drum.
Ud:	Middle Eastern lute. See Oud.
Unison:	Two more performers singing or playing the same part.
Unity in Diversity:	Indonesian motto which undergirds the national view on important issues, such as the reconciliation of cultural diversity with preservation of indigenous traditions.
Ustad:	A Muslim teacher, mentor, advisor. (Compare with Guru).
Vadi:	The central pitch of the raga, tonic.
Varnam:	The beginning song of a typical Karnatak recital.
Vedas:	The four ancient scriptures of Hinduism to which is attributed divine origin with music believed to be the fifth veda.
Vedic Chant:	Chants by Brahman priests from the Vedas.
Venu:	A Karnatak flute.
Verse-chorus form:	Verses alternating with choruses or refrains.

Vihuela:	A small Mexican guitar.
Vina:	A plucked, zither-like chordophone of the Karnatak tradition.
Vocables:	Syllables that are chanted or sung instead of words.
Wagon:	A Japanese zither with six strings.
Waki:	Supporting actor in the Japanese Noh drama.
Wayang kulit:	The Indonesian Shadow Puppet play.
Wayno:	Most common Andean mestizo genre.
Xiao Youmei:	Responsible for establishing and cultivating Chinese music Education in the early twentieth century.
Xiao:	A Chinese flute with six holes and end-blown.
Xipi:	A type of aria in Peking Opera, which is bright and happy as opposed to the seriousness and introspective nature of of the erhuang.
Xylophone:	A struck idiophone with tuned keys, sometimes resonated by gourds or pipes beneath the keys.
Yangqin:	A Chinese chordophone (dulcimer) played with two bamboo sticks.
Yayue:	Music of the Imperial Court of China, "elegant music." (Compare with Japanese gagaku.
Yeibechai:	A Navajo curing ceremony ("Night Chant") that lasts for nine days.
Yiddish:	A hybrid language combining Hebrew, Russian, German, Polish, as well as other languages and is spoken by a number of Jewish populations even today.
Yokyoku:	Noh Drama choral singing.
Yueqin:	A plucked four-stringed chordophone with a round sound box resembling a face.
Yunluo:	A set of suspended gongs from China,
Zarb:	Generically a drum but also another name for the Dombak.
Zheng:	A Chinese chordophone zither with moveable bridges with likenesses in Japan, Korea, and Mongolia.
Zither:	A chordophone with strings stretching from end to end of the sound board.
Zurkhaneh:	An Iranian gymnasium ("house of strength") where men meet, exercise, and listen to music.

Index

L

M

N

O